YOUNG LIONS

ORDINARY KIDS WITH EXTRAORDINARY COURAGE

BARBARA A. LEWIS

Deseret Book Company
Salt Lake City, Utah

Library of Congress Cataloging-in-Publication Data.

Lewis, Barbara A., 1943–
    Young Lions : ordinary kids with extraordinary courage / by
Barbara A. Lewis.
        p.   cm.
    ISBN 0-87579-771-7
    1. Mormon youth—United States—Biography—Juvenile literature.
    2. Heroes—United States—Biography—Juvenile literature.
    3. Courage—Juvenile literature. [1. Mormons—Biography.
    2. Courage. 3. Conduct of life.] I. Title.
    BX8693.L48   1993
    289.3'092'2—dc20   93-30361
    [B]   CIP
                                                                AC

Printed in the United States of America
10 9 8 7 6 5 4 3 2 1

CONTENTS

ACKNOWLEDGMENTS

I would like to acknowledge several people for lending their time and energy in sharing stories and expertise. President Bruce M. Lake offered many helpful suggestions and much assistance in obtaining international stories. Steven R. Mecham, former president of the Finland Helsinki East Mission, offered support and information regarding the Church in Estonia.

I would like to express appreciation to President Keith B. Knighton for his telephone time and to Phillip J. Bryson, professor at BYU, for his expertise on East Germany.

I wish to thank Helen Heaton, Carolyn Rasmus, Brad Wilcox, and Kathy Smith, who all offered leads to stories. The *Deseret News* also offered leads to many stories. Richard Romney, managing editor of the *New Era,* offered sound advice and a lead to a story.

I appreciate the help of Janice Dixon, who offered valuable editorial assistance. I would also like to acknowledge

Jetta Larson for her assistance in providing me time to write.

Most of all I would like to thank my husband, Larry, and our four children, Michael, Andrea, Christian, and Samuel, for their patience and support.

INTRODUCTION

When you think of demonstrations of faith or courage in the gospel, do you think of President Spencer W. Kimball when he endured the pain of festering boils covering his body? Do you think of the Prophet Joseph Smith's mighty faith in the Liberty Jail? Or do you think of Mary Fielding Smith asking for a blessing on her oxen so that she could continue across the plains? Do you go back further and think of Samuel the Lamanite prophesying on top of the Nephite wall, ignoring the shower of arrows? Or do you think of Nephi disguising himself as Laban in order to obtain the records, or of Mormon wandering alone and hiding in caves as he finished writing the history of his people?

You might think of any or all of them and realize, on further reflection, that all of these remarkable people were adults who displayed uncommon faith and courage. However, all of these individuals developed these qualities while they were children. Joseph Smith also demonstrated great courage as a boy, when he underwent, without anesthesia, an operation to remove an infected part of the bone in his leg.

King David spoke of young people: "Out of the mouth of babes and sucklings hast thou ordained strength." (Psalms 8:2.) And Isaiah: "And a little child shall lead them." (Isaiah 11:6.)

When the Savior visited the American continent, "he did teach and minister unto the children of the multitude . . . , and he did loose their tongues, and they did speak unto their fathers great and marvelous things, even greater than he had revealed unto the people; and he loosed their tongues that they could utter." (3 Nephi 26:14-15.)

What about youth? What about ordinary young people, those who don't necessarily make the front pages of newspapers? "Little children do have words given unto them many times, which confound the wise and the learned." (Alma 32:23.) "And not only this, but those things which never have been revealed from the foundation of the world, but have been kept hid from the wise and prudent, shall be revealed unto babes and sucklings in this, the dispensation of the fulness of times." (D&C 128:18.)

My experience teaching in public schools and in the Church has introduced me to many young heroes. I chose to highlight one of my students, Audrey Chase (pp. 69–78), and I am the teacher in that story. Some of the young people I write about are heroes of the moment, like young John Meranda (pp. 123–29), who saved a baby's life because of his quick thinking. Others have simply maintained the courage to be faithful in the face of opposition, like Silvanus Sebastian Pillay (pp. 81–90). Some of the heroes in this book have excelled in sports, academics, or music. Others have shared the gospel with friends, and one, Jaanus Silla, helped to open Estonia to the Church (pp. 177–86). Others have inspired those around them regardless of what their situations, whether they are in wheelchairs, in a homeless shelter, or on a deathbed.

I am not the same person I was before I wrote this book. My interviews with each of these children has magnified me, extended me, enriched me in a way that I cannot explain. To you, the reader, I can only say, meet each of these courageous Mormon youth through the pages of this book—these "children of light" (D&C 106:5) who, when faced with opposition, have been "bold as a lion" (Proverbs 28:1).

Brad Watson at age fourteen

Brigham Bowen at age fourteen

Brigham Bowen, left, and Brad Watson, right, by Brad's car

"YOU ARE MY FRIEND"

PARENTS

Darrell and Lana Watson

Scott and Annette Paxman Bowen

LOCATION OF STORY

Bellevue, Washington

Cold raindrops dripped from the tip of Brad's nose. Water drizzled in rivulets from the ends of his short blond hair and spilled under his collar, soaking the neck of his Metallica T-shirt. It didn't matter. He didn't even bother to snap his jacket.

He wasn't eager to go into Newport High in Bellevue, Washington, since he had cut his ninth-grade history class the past two days, and he would be behind. His teacher would demand assignments he didn't have. Maybe he'd just cut classes today too. He sought sanctuary in the school parking lot, smoking with his friends.

"Hey, look who's coming," one of the boys said, pointing the back of his hand in the direction of the early morning seminary students just arriving at school. "It's Brigham Bowen, himself. Brigham, the Great Fag. Right, Brad?"

Brigham Bowen hardly appeared to notice the group of boys. Maybe the back of his neck flinched. Maybe he

1

broke stride, but if he did, it was only for a second. Brad couldn't really tell in the gray rain, but he only half smiled at his friends. His eyes were drawn like a magnet to Brigham, who strolled by in a cotton shirt, a nice leather jacket, and Top-sider shoes. Brigham always appeared to be in a hurry, as if he knew where he was going. Yeah, Brigham was strange, all right, but something about him—a briskness, a sense of confidence—attracted Brad, and he wished he knew what made the strange boy tick.

Brad looked down at his own jacket. It was covered with graffiti and rock band slogans he and his friends had painted. In a futile gesture, he brushed splashes of water from his shoulders and down the burned sleeves. He had set the arms of his jacket on fire several times, mostly out of curiosity just to watch the reactions of others.

Brad searched his friends' faces. They gazed back with empty, glazed looks while puffing away on their cigarettes held between stained fingers. Brad rolled the cigarette between his thumb and index finger. He noted that his hands weren't stained yet.

Brad dropped the cigarette and smashed it with a black Nike, though he didn't really know why. "Got to hit the classes today," he apologized to his surprised friends. Then he made up an excuse: "My mom's been raggin' at me." As the bell clanged, Brad took the steps three at a time into Newport High.

He suffered through English and math and wrote down the missing assignments. He thought about the gossipy rumors they had spread about Brigham Bowen. How could Brigham stand it? Like at the football game against Issaquah a month ago:

Brad had plopped down on the bleachers with his friends a few rows behind Kevin and Brigham, who were laughing and joking with a bunch of their foxy girlfriends. Kevin had draped an arm loosely over one thin girl's shoulder. He chatted and grinned under a worn baseball cap smashed down over rusty-copper hair. The girl seemed to ignore Kevin and glanced sideways at Brigham. Did she think Brigham was handsome? Brad didn't know how to judge what girls thought. He looked at Brigham, his blond hair, blue eyes. He obviously wasn't tall, like him, and he didn't look like a jock.

What did Brad know about this strange new kid? Brigham played soccer. He was a Mormon, one of about seventy in the school, and someone had said that he had won a lead part in the school play, *The Foreigner*, although he was only a freshman. Yeah, he was a "foreigner" all right.

The thin girl jabbed Brigham in the ribs, and her cheeks glowed.

Yeah, Brad thought, she thinks he's handsome. And then Brad began taunting. "Hey, Brigham Bowen, we've heard a lot about you."

Brigham only ignored them.

Brad and his friends dug in deeper. "Kevin's a gay fag," one of Brad's friends called out, "and everyone knows it. You both are."

Brigham stuck up for his friend, yelling loudly, "You're off base. It isn't true. Who are you going to believe?"

Kevin just pulled his baseball cap down further over his eyes, while Brigham did most of the talking.

Brad guessed Brigham would have faced them nose to nose if they hadn't been separated by three splintery rows of bleachers. There was another weird thing about this Brigham. He seemed to shrug off the abuse heaped on himself, just as he casually brushed their cigarette smoke away from his face, but he stood up for his friend.

Brad had seen the same thing happen several times in the halls at Newport. The last time it was outside the lunchroom. Some guys had hurled insults at Brigham and

Kevin, and Brigham had argued, but again, only to defend Kevin and not himself. Brad had come close to mocking Brigham too, but he had stopped, the cruel words trapped in his throat. Curious about this strange boy, Brad had almost spoken to Brigham, but Brigham had hustled off, his bag thrown over his shoulder, in his usual hurry, always aimed in some direction.

Brad was attracted to strength. He was a powerful swimmer, and he had hung numerous ribbons and swimming medals on the two bulletin boards in his bedroom. He swam for Newport and the USA teams, practicing before and after school and sometimes in the evening.

Brad knew Brigham had strength too, but he guessed it was different—something quite different. For some crazy reason, the next day in his art class, Brad asked Kevin for Brigham's phone number.

"Why do you want that?" Kevin stared at Brad. Kevin's hair fell over one eye in a salmon-colored wave. "You going to harass him at home too?"

Brad snickered. "No, I just thought maybe . . . " He paused. "I thought maybe I'd ask him to see a movie next Sunday."

"You're joking."

"No, what can it hurt?" Maybe he could look beneath Brigham's smooth smile, see what was underneath.

Kevin laughed. "You'll never get Brigham to go," he said, clicking his retainer against his teeth. "You're wasting your time."

"What do you mean?"

"Because it's Sunday. Bet you Brigham won't go on a Sunday."

Kevin was right. When Brad called him, Brigham spoke friendly enough on the phone, although he paused and sounded a little surprised at the phone call before saying he had other things he needed to do. Brad wasn't sure if he refused because it was Sunday, or more likely, because Brigham hated him.

Brad had his answer the following Monday in the school library. Brigham looked at Brad and marched right over in his direction. Their eyes met. Brad half expected a confrontation, a "how-come-you're-such-a-jerk" statement, and he mentally prepared a comeback. He should never have called him.

To his surprise, Brigham sat down at the table next to Brad and smiled. "So, how was the movie?" He handed him a handful of sour candies.

"Uh, okay," Brad stumbled. "It was a—just a movie." He laughed, and he knew then that Brigham had forgiven him for his cruel taunting.

Brad called Brigham that night on the phone. He made up a question about a math equation, and he called him the next night, and the next, and regularly after that.

"Hey," Brigham finally said over the phone, sounding just slightly annoyed. "When do you have time to study?" Then Brad heard him laugh. Brigham must have covered the mouthpiece, for Brad only heard muffled conversation. Then Brigham spoke again. "Look, why don't you just come over and meet my gang? My mom insists." He chuckled again. "She wants to check you out."

Brad accepted, and after that he came over most weekends and practically adopted Brigham's family too. The rumors that Brad had helped spread at school about Brigham and Kevin faded, then died away.

When both boys picked up their midterm grades at Newport, they discussed what they had gotten. Brigham had 4.0 again and grinned confidently. Brad had some high grades, but he also had several Ds that could turn to Fs if he didn't set to work.

"How come some of your grades are so high, and you're failing others?" Brigham pointed at a D.

Brad slouched on the couch in Brigham's front room. "I guess it's because I keep cutting the classes." A car's horn tooted outside, and he heard a siren scream in the distance.

"I don't know how you can do that. You're only hurting yourself." Brigham smiled. "I'll bet if you started attending classes and paying attention, you could come up with a 3.0 by the end of the year. I'll help you."

Brad stared at Brigham.

"Every time you call, I'm going to ask you if you've done your homework, and if you haven't, we won't talk. Okay?"

Man, Brad thought, this is some strange guy. He doesn't smoke, doesn't drink, doesn't do drugs. He sticks up for his friend and does his homework. Brad shrugged, snickered, and nodded his head in agreement.

Brad went home, grabbed two slices of bread, and reached for the phone, but he remembered and stopped. He got out his books and spread them across the table. Two hours later, he swept his completed assignments into a pile. Then he leaned back on the kitchen chair with his hands folded behind his head. It felt good to be finished.

He reached in his backpack and pulled out a cigarette, one he had bummed from a friend, then tossed it into a garbage can. He would never need one of those again.

Over the next month, Brad's grades started to recover. He began to hang out with Brigham so much that he slipped away from his old gang. It wasn't really planned. It just happened. He respected Brigham's parents a lot, and he wondered how much they knew about the old rumors he had spread.

Brad continued to drop by Brigham's house on weekends throughout the winter and spring. The house usually smelled of blueberry muffins or pot roast. Brad started to eat with the Bowens, too: Brigham, his parents, and Brigham's younger brothers, Nathan and Jeremy. Everyone helped each other with dishes. Brigham often played the piano, while his younger brothers wrestled on the floor, and sometimes all four of them toppled across the rug.

During the weekdays Brigham's bedroom vibrated with the sounds of rock music, but on Sundays the boys listened to classical music, like Pachelbel's Canon in D, Handel's *Water Music,* or Chopin's preludes.

In the evenings Brad often plopped down on a wooden stool in the Bowen kitchen to ask questions, mostly of Brigham and his mother. He asked about the Church, about its stand on morality, about faith, and about how you can know God is real.

One afternoon Brad asked Brigham if he had ever done anything bad, something he felt really sorry for. Brigham leaned back, balancing on two chair legs. "Oh, sure."

"Like what?"

While Brigham scratched his head, his mother, chimed in, "He used to TP houses."

Brad's smile screwed to one side, while Brigham's face reddened.

She continued, "And he had a book fight in the library once, and shoved trash down the stairs at school—"

"You can quit any time now," Brigham interrupted, cocking his head at his mother.

"Are those the *worst* things you've done? Come on," Brad said, smirking.

"Well, I felt awful, and I had to help the custodian during lunch for a while."

Brad rubbed his hair and chuckled, "Oh, what an idiot!"

"Well, I have been called worse things, you know."
Brigham grinned.

Brad cleared his throat, "Well, yeah." It was the first
time in months that Brigham had hinted at the old
rumors. Brad knew he had to get rid of the extra baggage
of guilt. He also feared it might mark the end of their
friendship, but he swallowed and said to Mrs. Bowen,
"You know I'm the 'one,' don't you?"

"The 'one' what?" Brigham's mother asked.

He looked at Brigham and back at his mother. "The
'one' who started . . . all the rumors about Brigham and
Kevin. It was pretty innocent at first. You know both you
and Kevin were new guys at Newport. Well, one day in
history, Kevin had been acting like a jerk, so I just called
him a 'fag.' Other guys heard it and believed it, and the
name just sort of stuck."

Brad paused. He couldn't really read Mrs. Bowen's
expression, but her lips pulled tight. Now that he had
gone this far, there was no backing up, like those times
when his tires would get ripped if he tried to reverse, he
thought. "We started calling Brigham the same thing, and
people thought it was true, because he was Kevin's friend
and stood up for him. Then the rumors just kept spreading."

He stared at Brigham and then at Mrs. Bowen's large,
disbelieving eyes. Brad's stomach took a somersault. "You
mean Brigham never told you?"

She caught her breath and shook her head before she
turned her back toward him.

Brad rushed to add, "But Brigham just blew it all
away. He never acted like it bothered him."

Brigham's mother spoke softly, her back still toward
him. "He didn't brush it off so easily, Brad. Sometimes
when he came home, he was totally crushed. It's about
the worst kind of abuse I can think of."

"Yeah, I would rather be beaten up in a back alley behind the school." Brigham playfully punched Brad in the ribs.

She cleared her throat. "I just have to say this. Why would anyone spread such terrible lies about another person?" She turned and stared at Brad.

Brad lowered his eyes and swallowed.

Brigham straightened his shoulders and said in defense of his friend, "I know who I am. I guess it doesn't really matter what anyone says so long as I know the things they say aren't true."

Brad couldn't believe this strange friend of his. His throat thickened, and then he brushed a fist against Brigham's shoulder. "Especially if he's an idiot." They both laughed, and Brad looked at Mrs. Bowen, awaiting her judgment.

She reached into Brad's bag of sour candies, popped a couple into her mouth, and grimaced.

Brad blew between his teeth. He knew then that Brigham's mother wouldn't hold it against him either.

Many afternoons they talked until the lights flipped on surrounding the Seattle Temple. He could see it from Brigham's kitchen window, and Brad often leaned restless hands on the window ledge and stared at Angel Moroni atop the spire a half mile away. The temple looked so peaceful: the stained-glass windows, the fountain, the evergreen trees surrounding it. Brad knew what kind of life he wanted. "I'm just too scared of the chase," he confided in Brigham. "What would my parents say?"

Near the end of June, Brigham invited Brad to come with him to a stake dance. Brigham's parents were in charge of all of the youth activities in the Renton Washington North Stake.

"You're kidding, right? What would I wear?" Brad asked.

Brigham said, "Oh, some nicer pants and a button-down shirt, that kind of thing."

"I've never owned a shirt with a collar in my life," he protested. "Besides, I'm not even sure I can dance."

Brad stayed away from the first dance, but he sat all alone on the edge of his bed that evening, wondering what he was missing. He showed up on the Bowen's doorstep before the second dance, wearing brand new pants and a long-sleeve dress shirt. He ran his finger inside the stiff collar. "Do you ever get used to these?" he asked.

By the end of July, while Brad's house was getting painted, he asked if he could stay with Brigham for a few days. The Bowens were happy to have him, but they told him they were all attending youth conference that week, and Brad agreed to go to youth conference with Brigham as part of the deal.

Brigham's mother helped a youth committee write a play for the conference, *The Valiant Generation,* about a Mormon boy who has a best friend who is not a Mormon. Brad watched Brigham and his friends in the play practices and after the rehearsals as they laughed, jabbed ribs, and joked. They teased Brad too and insisted that he join them. After the play Brad and Brigham attended workshops, dances, and games.

The conference ended with a testimony meeting. Brigham stood and spoke about how grateful he was for his family, friends, and the Church. Almost all the actors in the play told of their love for each other, and Brad's eyes stung as he listened.

Then Brigham's mom stood. She talked about how important it was to include others. When she expressed her love for Brigham and asked his forgiveness for an argument they had had the day before, Brad lowered his face and blinked back tears.

Brad listened, and his chest began to burn with a warm, peaceful feeling. He wanted to stand and say something too, but he didn't know quite how to express himself. Later, another boy at youth conference, Travis Hall, asked Brad if he wanted the missionary discussions, and Brad said, "Yes."

Over several weeks, he heard all six discussions at the Halls' home. Brigham attended once when the missionaries invited him, and Brad began attending church each week with Brigham. Brad's own closet grew more crowded with additional church clothes—nice shirts and slacks and even dress shoes.

Brad felt a warm, safe feeling whenever the missionaries talked about the Holy Ghost and about Jesus. When he finished each meeting, he called Brigham to ask him what he thought of life after death, the Holy Ghost, or morality.

Brad's parents had always supported his interests. So after the second discussion, he told his mom what he was doing. She came to the fourth missionary discussion. Afterward, she said she wasn't interested herself, but she wouldn't stand in his way. He also told his dad about the discussions, but Brad was nervous to tell him his plan to be baptized, because he was afraid his dad might be disappointed in him.

"What should I do?" he asked Brigham.

"Well, you have to get your parents' permission. I always think it's easier to just walk right up and ask something. Be straight forward," Brigham suggested.

Finally, a week before his baptismal date, Brad squared his shoulders and marched up to his dad. Mr. Watson was lounging on the couch watching a football game, and Brad blurted, "I'm getting baptized Sunday. You can come if you want."

His dad started to chuckle and then asked, "What time?" Brad then knew his dad wouldn't be angry or disappointed with him.

Brad was baptized October 20, the Sunday following his sixteenth birthday. One of the elders baptized him, and Brigham's father confirmed him. Brigham gave one of the talks. He said, "You and I will always be friends no matter what. But you must always have the commitment to follow the pathway that leads you to light and Heavenly Father's love."

Brad went home and hung a picture of the Seattle Temple on his newly painted wall, right next to a Guns and Roses poster. He began reading the Book of Mormon each night before he went to bed.

He later confided in Mrs. Bowen, "Now I have a 3.2 grade point average, and it's climbing." He was munching one of her blueberry muffins at the kitchen table. "And I want to go on a mission." He grew thoughtful. "You know, lots of people have helped me. I respect Travis, and he was big on talking to me about stuff at all the discussions, and I respect all the Mormon youth." Brigham's mom placed another muffin on his plate and a hand on his shoulder.

"But Brigham is my friend. He's the one I watched and the one who made me want to change. He's the greatest person I've ever met in my life."

Jeff Clayton, left;
Becky Clayton, right

Becky Clayton with her
team's state high school
championship trophy

Becky Clayton in quarterfinals play-off game at Assembly Hall

BECKY CLAYTON

KEEP YOUR HEAD UP

PARENTS

George W. Clayton, Sr., and Sevenia Bracklin Clayton (deceased)

LOCATION OF STORY

Sullivan, Illinois

As dawn's light splintered through the bedroom shutters in Sullivan, Illinois, six-year-old Becky's eyes popped open. Jeff would have come home in the middle of the night on leave from the Air Force. Although Jeff was thirteen years older, he functioned as her hero and her guide, and she thought he would always be there for her.

She leaped out of bed and raced up the stairs to Jeff's bedroom, threw open the door, and pounced on his sleeping back. She knifed her arm between his neck and the sheets and bear hugged him. "Wake up," she commanded. "Let's play. I've been waiting for you. I went to bed early so I could get up and see you."

Jeff groaned and opened one eye to look at his watch. "Five-fifteen! You ought to be shot." His dark hair contrasted with the white sheets. All five of the children had inherited some of their mother's striking Sioux features.

"Guess what? Guess? I learned to kick a football . . . far . . . like you showed me." She expected him to smile, hug her, lift her on his shoulders, but instead, he just lay there still as a brick. She shook his shoulders, but he didn't move. He wasn't even breathing. "Jeff! Jeff!" Her cheeks prickled with fear as she tried to turn his motionless body over.

Suddenly Jeff reached up, grabbed her in a headlock, and pinned her down. She squealed and wriggled while he tickled her tummy and blew loud rumbles against her neck.

When she stopped giggling and caught her breath, she said, "Jeff, don't do that ever again."

"Do what, Fonzie? You mean this?" He rubbed his sandpaper whiskers on her neck.

"No. No," she squealed. "Don't ever play . . . dead. Don't ever, ever . . . die . . . ," and she choked with laughter under his scratchy chin.

Jeff taught her to catch a football, to kick, and to run with the speed of the wind. He carted her piggyback on his 6' 2" frame against another brother, George, so she could score touchdowns. She threw her dolls under the bed and ran short-haired and dirty-faced through hay and bean fields with a football cradled in her arm.

She counted the days between each of Jeff's visits. With all of Jeff's expert coaching, Becky qualified for the seventh-grade state track meet, running for Sullivan Junior High, even though she was only eleven.

On that day of the meet, she stretched her long legs, pressing against the starting block on the track, and waited for the gun to fire for the hundred-yard dash. But how could she do it without Jeff? He taught her how to run, and he had promised that he would be there to watch her.

She recalled her brother's voice on the phone the night before, calling from Arizona, where he now worked in construction. "Look, Fonz, I can't get off work. Now don't cry.

You're a tough girl. It's just too far to come, but don't worry. You're the best. Just remember to keep your head up high."

She instinctively pulled her head up, swallowed some tears, and rotated her shoulders to loosen up, but she felt as if someone had ripped the rug from beneath her feet.

And then she heard her name, "Becky. Fonzie. I'm here."

Fifty yards ahead on the side of the track, Jeff was sprinting toward her. He had come. He had flown all the way from Tucson, Arizona, just to watch her, and then the tears did sting her eyes.

Bang!

Becky dashed forward. Jeff ran along beside her on the grass, cheering, "Go, Fonz, go. You can do it. You're the best. There's no one better."

With Jeff running on the sideline, Becky's feet barely touched the ground.

She earned a fifth-place award in that race and second place in the two-hundred-yard dash. When she received her ribbons, Becky gazed at Jeff, his Adonis build and dark complexion. As the judge handed her a ribbon, she saw her brother's eyebrows arch in anticipation. She locked eyes with him. He winked at her, and Becky's cheeks tingled. She hardly saw the ribbon.

Then Jeff rewarded her with a ride on his motorcycle. She slipped on Jeff's dark shades and thumbed her nose at all her boyfriends, who would have given all their baseball cards for just one ride. She hugged Jeff's chest and squealed, "Yahoo." Then she rested her head on his back. "Thanks for coming. I couldn't have done that without you."

"Yes, you could have, Fonzie." Jeff's laughter flew past her ears. "I might not always be around, but you don't need me."

"Yes, I do." Becky squeezed him tighter. "You'll always be around. You have to."

"Nah, I told you that you could do it yourself, but then you've never listened a whole lot to my advice."

"Yes, I do. You think I don't listen, but I always do."

Jeff's motorcycle zipped up the driveway to the two-story house. "You listen when it's something you want to hear," he said as he pinched her cheek. "I told you not to play tackle football, and you played anyway with George's high school friends. Remember?"

"Yeah, yeah! And I broke my thumb and my arm." She grinned. "But that's just because I'm such a stick." She frowned at her long, thin legs.

"Hey, those sticks can run faster than a speeding bullet." He pulled Becky off the motorcycle and carted her over his shoulder into the house as she giggled and squealed.

Jeff continued to come home at every possible chance. In November, when Becky was in seventh grade, he returned home for Thanksgiving just as the first frost varnished the grass. She had discouraging news and cried as soon as she saw him. Would he be disappointed in her?

"I hurt my back in the long jump at the high school, and now I can't do long jumps anymore." She buried her face in his chest.

"It's okay, Fonzie." He patted her on the back. "You don't need to cry."

Becky quickly dried her tears so that Jeff wouldn't think she was a baby. Why couldn't she hold back tears? "But I can still run. I've been playing basketball, like you did in high school." She looked at him hopefully.

"Great idea. I'd love to see you become a great basketball player, and you will." He pinched her nose and said, "Because I'm going to teach you every secret I know. Grab a ball."

The tears dried in streaks on her cheeks while she charged after the basketball.

Jeff instructed her every day for the two weeks he was home. He shared all his pointers on shooting, jumping, rebounding, and playing defense. "When a shot goes up, you have to block out. Get your man out of the way so you can rebound," he told her.

She memorized his words, tried to practice them, and sometimes argued with him.

The following March, when Becky was nearly thirteen, she sat in the doctor's office, her throat burning as if it had been scorched with a branding iron. Because she was now taller than both her mother and father, she slumped down to rest her head against her mother's shoulder. The sage her mother had burned in her bedroom to cure her infection hadn't helped. She sneezed. She was probably allergic to it.

Suddenly her sister, Kathy, burst through the door of the doctor's office. She stood there with large owl-like eyes, panting. "Mom, it's Jeff."

Becky caught her breath. The draft from the open door chilled her shoulders, and she shivered.

"Jeff's been in an awful accident."

Becky grabbed her mother's hand. Not Jeff. No. He would be okay she told herself, trying to drown her old fears that something might happen to her hero. Although her family were all Mormons, suddenly she wished they had all been sealed to each other in the temple.

The physician from the Tucson Medical Center didn't give them any details but only indicated that Jeff had been seriously injured on the construction site where he worked. Becky's mom and her sister and brother, Jackie and George, flew immediately to Tucson. Becky was forced to stay home with her dad and Kathy to wait for their phone call. Becky felt numb and walked around in a mechanical, windup way. She didn't want to go to school. When the phone rang in the evening, she rushed to answer it. She finally heard the details from Jackie and her mom.

Jeff had been working on demolition at a construction site. Operating on a tight budget, the company had ignored safety rules and neglected to shut off the electricity on that block. Jeff was on the controls in a cab, operating a crane with a co-worker sitting in the gondola above.

Suddenly the machine had malfunctioned, and the crane started to collapse. The gondola tipped over backwards and began falling toward some electrical wires below. Although Jeff had sat safely grounded, he bounded from the cab, sprinted across the ground, and leaped onto the gondola while it was still eight feet in the air. He pulled himself up and shoved his co-worker safely out the other side, but as Jeff tried to jump to safety, the gondola hit the wires. A galvanic explosion of sparks struck the gondola, searing ten thousand volts of electricity through his shuddering body. The jolt hurled him two hundred feet away.

The man Jeff had saved grabbed Jeff's body. Jeff's lungs and heart had stopped, so the man punched Jeff's chest and blew air into his lungs. Although Jeff remained unconscious, his heart began to thump, and his lungs sucked in air until the paramedics arrived with oxygen. The ambulance sped to Tucson Medical Center where Jeff remained in a coma.

For two weeks, Jeff lay in a coma. At the end of that time, Jeff's mom decided to take him off the breathing machine. She explained to the family that Jeff had once told her that if anything ever happened to him, he would not want to be kept alive with machines. He didn't want to live like a vegetable in the ground that couldn't move. She told the rest of the family to fly down, because once they took the life-support systems off Jeff, they would need to be there to say good-bye.

What did it mean to be a vegetable? How could Jeff's accident make him a vegetable? Becky couldn't concentrate on her homework, nor could she stay focused on her dad's instructions. She just watched his lips move.

"Becky! You're not listening," his voice called.

Was he saying something to her? Yes. Pack a bag.

A numbness filled her chest as she, her dad, and Kathy flew to Tucson. Finally they stood outside Jeff's hospital room. Becky took a deep breath and walked in. She saw Jeff covered by white sheets with tubes connecting his body to machines. She remembered the image of the vegetable. Was this what it meant? She thought of the bean fields at home and how tiny beans sprouted roots for nourishment. Jeff's tubes reminded her of roots sprouting from Jeff's body, and she grew dizzy. His eyes were taped shut, and his burly body trembled and convulsed in shudders of pain.

Becky panted for breath, and she seemed to be spinning in circles. No, she was standing still—the room was whirling around in a tornado. Jeff, his bed, the IV poles spun around while her parents' arms reached toward her. Then someone turned out the lights, and she dropped to the floor.

She awoke in a hospital chair with her mother patting her cheeks. Jackie was rubbing her arms. "You fainted, Becky. Just sit still for a minute."

Her eyes were still glued on Jeff, and she thought he was speaking to her. But no, his eyes were still taped shut, and his lips were not moving. In her mind she could

imagine Jeff's words: "You're a tough girl, Becky. You don't
need to cry. Listen to me this time. Keep your head up."
For the first time in her life she didn't cry, because she
couldn't. She had to be tough for Jeff and decided she
would never cry again.

Miraculously, when the physician removed the life-
support equipment, Jeff continued to breathe on his own.
Becky's parents flew him to the Rehabilitation Institute of
Chicago. After four months with Jeff still in a coma, they
brought him home and set him up in a hospital bed in
the front room. As nurses themselves, both Becky's mom
and Jackie were qualified to care for him with the help of
visiting nurses.

Only Becky's mother seemed able to communicate
with him. She could get him to bat his eyelashes sometimes in response to what she asked.

For a while Becky's body was a hollow drum. She
didn't cry and couldn't concentrate well enough to think.
She moved about in a stupor, often staying away from
Jeff's bed, from this stranger's shell who wasn't really
Jeff.

She saw her mother and father whispering together,
looking at Jeff, then at her. Her mother shook her head
and clicked her tongue.

"Here, child, eat. You look as skinny as a bamboo
pole." Her mother pushed potatoes, chicken, and fry bread
in front of her, but Becky took only a few bites and then
poked her fork at the food.

"Come on, Fonz, let's shoot a few baskets," George
said, bouncing a basketball in front of her.

She hardly heard his words as she walked by. It
seemed to her as if she were in a vacuum and everything
outside her body belonged to another world.

After a few weeks, it hit her. There was Jeff, and here
she was. He wasn't moving, and she could run. It was

Jeff, and he had left her. For some reason she recalled a memory of Jeff, back when she was small. Her family had driven to Aunt Sissy's house in North Dakota to attend a powwow with her mother's people in the Hidatsa Tribe. She had never seen one before, and the chanting and dancing of the men with painted streaks on their faces terrified her. But Jeff had pulled her near and pointed at the buffalo ambling slowly through knee-high grass. Suddenly she had felt warm, safe, unafraid, and the buffalo had become her favorite animal.

Becky stared at Jeff's helpless body now. She walked slowly up to his side, lifted his broad hand in hers, and stroked it. "I need you, Jeff. I need you to come back. Remember the powwow when you . . . "

He looked straight ahead.

She batted her eyes. Even as she spoke, something told her he wouldn't be there to scatter her fears or to teach her anymore, but it wasn't his fault, and he hadn't left her completely. She could almost hear his answer, remember his words: "Listen to me, Fonz. I would love to see you become a great basketball player . . . Remember what I said . . . You know how to do it." Jeff hadn't left her. She still had his advice, and it constantly played over and over in her head.

She awoke the next morning with the sun burning through the window on her face. She stretched and felt warmth down to her toes. She had to get moving, if only for Jeff. Father in Heaven would help her. She spent the day shooting baskets, her jaw set, her eyes thin, determined slits. She couldn't stop as she drove the ball again and again for a layup, never quite satisfied with her performance, and she prayed for help. The weeks and months stretched into a year as she hustled beneath the basket, driving, making layups, perfecting her skill, and she felt more connected to Jeff.

In August, a little more than two years after Jeff's accident, her mom and dad, Kathy, and Becky (and later Jackie) went to the temple to be sealed. They received special permission from the First Presidency to have a proxy stand in for Jeff. After the sealing, Becky told her mother, "Now we're really connected to Jeff."

Becky's long bony legs rounded and grew until she reached six feet tall in high school. She let her hair grow long. It fell in dark, feathered wisps to her shoulders. Guys stopped and stared, whistled at her, and she impressed them with her skillful shots at the basket.

One morning Becky went into the front room and took Jeff's hand in hers as she often did. Always unresponsive, his eyes were open, but he stared straight ahead. She stroked the pronounced veins in his hand, held his hand to her cheek, then kissed it. "Jeff, I have a deep, burning testimony of the Church. It's the gospel that has held us together through this," she told him. He stared ahead, his face vacant and cold as an empty freezer.

"Jeff, I've made the Sullivan basketball team." Was he still inside his body? She wished he could hear her and react some way. "I'm playing basketball just like you."

Becky did play. She started each game during her high school career as the center. Before each game she kneeled at Jeff's bedside and prayed. In her junior year they lost by only one point to Teotopolis High School, the team that later won the state crown.

In her senior year as captain of the team, she averaged eighteen points and fourteen rebounds per game. All the while Jeff's instructions ran through her mind like a tape recorder as she darted around the court.

Spectators watched with hushed voices when Becky— as the only Mormon in the 330 members of the student body—pulled her team around her before each game. They sat in a circle with their feet touching in the middle and holding hands, forming a fearless floret. Then, as captain of her team, she led them in prayer. She prayed that they would be strong, that they could accept the outcome, that they would be safe, that Coach Scott Thomas would have the wisdom to instruct them, and that they would play well.

In the evenings after the games, she would take Jeff's hand in hers and tell him everything that had happened. She asked his advice, and even though he stared straight ahead, she knew what he would answer if he could.

Becky led the Lady Redskins in a spotless 35–0 winning season. She dedicated each game to Jeff as she jogged onto the court. Everyone knew it. Teammates sponged her strength and determined to play harder.

Becky was selected as Player of the Year in the small school division and Co-Player of the Year in both the small and large school balloting. DePaul University's coach, Doug Bruno, considered her to be one of the "top two high school prospects in the country." Scores of nationally ranked women's basketball programs tried to entice her to attend their universities.

When the Lady Redskins won the Illinois Class A state championship against Seneca in Champaign, a fire truck escorted the team through town. People lined the streets, waved red and black pom-poms and cheered. The entire community rallied in the high school gym. Becky was patted, squeezed, and carted on shoulders while the deafening cheers rang in her ears.

Then she left the rumpus behind and slipped home. In the contrasting silence of her home, the squeaking door seemed to shout as she opened it. She walked slowly to Jeff, who was propped up in a chair. She hugged him and whispered, "You think I didn't listen to you, that I didn't always understand and hear what you said, but I did, Jeff. I heard every word." She sniffed. "I wish I knew if you could hear me." Then she pulled the state championship medal from around her neck and placed it slowly over her brother's head. "Here, Jeff. This is for you."

Then Jeff shut his eyes, and she distinctly heard him sigh.

POSTSCRIPT: Becky decided to stay in Illinois to be close to Jeff and her family. She played basketball at Millikin University in Decatur, a half hour from her home. She planned to become an optometrist.

Left to right in back row: Elders Santos, Anderson,
and Penrod. Middle: Daniel Vargas. Front: Elder Michael Moore

DANIEL SILVEIRA VARGAS

CONVERSION IN BRAZIL

PARENTS
Decio Azevedo (deceased) and Beatrix Silveira Vargas

LOCATION OF STORY
Porto Alegre, Brazil

(Written by author with translation assistance
of Elder Michael Moore)

Seventeen-year-old Daniel Vargas lurched down the maze of winding streets and back alleys on his way home to the Cefer area of Porto Alegre, Brazil. His head felt fluffy from too much drinking, and he knew he shouldn't be stumbling around alone at 3:30 A.M. A voice inside told him that this was not the type of life he should be leading, but he buried the thought.

His mother had warned him to be more careful. "There are too many thugs," she had said, shaking her finger in his face.

He passed a bar on the corner where teenagers sang and danced wildly under a sagging awning. Rock music rumbled through the streets, while an odor of liquor mixed with a stale belch from a manhole cover. Daniel wanted to join the party, but he had promised his mother that he would take a turn caring for his mentally disabled sister, Gorda, in the morning.

A Volkswagen with a police siren wailing screeched to a halt beside the gutter, and Daniel teetered unsteadily as the police jumped out and grabbed a man four feet away from him who was waiting for the bus. The police ripped open the man's jacket and yanked out a package that looked as if it contained marijuana, set it on fire, and dropped it on the ground. Then one policeman punched the guy in the stomach and threw him in the patrol car.

Daniel backed away and hurried up the street. He didn't want to tangle with the police any more than with the thugs who lurked in shadowed alleys.

His head started to clear as he passed the Ipiranga River, and Daniel inhaled a mixture of car exhaust fumes, industrial smoke, and fresh bread from a bakery already raising dough for the morning. He headed toward the hill to his home, passing tiny cement houses stuck together with common walls that formed winding alleyways. Orange tile roofs rolled over the pastel houses without a break. A door sagged open, spilling smoke, laughter, and accordion strains into the street.

As Daniel wound higher through the labyrinth of streets, shadows and silence settled around him. Occasionally he stumbled over tufts of weeds pushing up through dirt and broken walks. For some reason he remembered as a child how frightened he had been of monsters he saw in the cinema. Then he heard something. It was like the tinkle of tin on the street. His heart raced, and he wiped sweat from his forehead.

Turning around the next bend, he spied a man hunkered over in a dark doorway. The man didn't seem to notice him, but Daniel swerved to the middle of the narrow street and broke into a jog. As he stumbled around the next alley, he paused and listened for the thud of shoes on the broken cobblestones but heard nothing. He heaved a deep sigh of relief and slowed his pace.

Then it happened. Out of nowhere Daniel heard a quick shuffle of feet. An arm grabbed him around the neck and slammed him against the wall of a cement house. The butt end of a gun smashed into his cheek. Daniel's temples pulsed as he grabbed the metal security bar on the window for balance.

"Give me your shoes," a husky voice demanded. The man jabbed the revolver into Daniel's stomach. His dark eyes glowed. His breath smelled of sour liquor, and his T-shirt reeked of sweat.

Daniel's voice shook. "Sure! Here, take them." He kicked off his tennis shoes.

"And your jacket." The man grabbed Daniel's arm.

Daniel eased out of his denim jacket, first one arm, then the other. He didn't want to make any sudden moves with the gun denting his stomach. His heart throbbed in his throat, while the small man stuffed the goods under his arm and then zagged off into the shadows.

Daniel leaned against the house, rubbed his hands over his dark, curly hair, and caught his breath before dashing home.

Later his mother reinforced her warning. "It isn't safe in the streets, Daniel. You should not do this thing—this roaming around at night." She cut potatoes into a large black pot in their tiny four-by-four-foot kitchen.

"Oh, don't worry so much, Mother," Daniel said, but inside, his chest trembled whenever he thought of the attack.

She shook her fist. "If your father was alive, he would knock some sense in you."

Daniel remembered his father vividly and all the times he had sat in his lap while his dad told the familiar story of Mr. No-Nose and snatched at Daniel's nose. His father had died of a heart attack when Daniel was twelve.

He had suddenly stopped breathing and was gone, and Daniel still felt needles in his heart when he thought of it.

"You are the oldest son living at home," his mother had told him after the funeral. "Now you must become a man. You must get a job as your six older brothers and sisters have. They do not live at home, but they still help. We all give to the family, and we all share."

"I'll help, Mother."

"Your father left us some support money, but we all need to work."

"I'll find jobs. I can run errands for businesses, and I can find other things." Daniel had known it would take the combined efforts of all the children to keep the family going financially. His mother had to stay home to care for Gorda and his younger brother Rafael, who was also mentally disabled. In a few years, his sister Vivi, three years younger, would also look for jobs.

Daniel had found many odd jobs to help his family, but as he had grown older, he spent more and more of his evenings with his friends, prowling around at night through bars and back alleys.

A few days after the mugging, his fear slipped away, and he returned to his carefree partying into the early morning hours. "I am happy," he told himself. "Life is slow and good." But when he said it, he paused and thought, because inside he still felt something was missing.

He was mugged two more times in the night as a teenager. One time the thug stole his watch. The other time, the robber snatched at his glasses, but Daniel protested, "I can't see without them. They won't fit your eyes anyway. What else can I give you?" The thief demanded the pants right off Daniel's body.

When he returned home, Daniel slipped quietly into his bed before his mother could notice and throw her hands in the air and scold him. Even though he was dead tired, for a long time he couldn't slow his beating heart and go to sleep.

Daniel was nineteen years old when he boarded the rear of the dented city bus. He was traveling to his job in a business firm, where he answered phones, filed papers, and did other office work in order to save money to attend the Porto Alegrense College and to help his family. He hoisted his baggy pants held in place by a wide leather belt.

"*Oi,*" an American voice said.

Daniel looked up at two enormously tall young men who had to duck their heads to avoid hitting the ceiling of the bus. "*Oi,*" Daniel answered. He decided the blond young men must be Americans and were at least six feet four inches tall.

"Where are you from?" Daniel asked in English. "Are you Americans?"

Elder Ron Chatfield answered, "Yes, I'm from California, and this guy's from Utah." He elbowed his companion, Mike Moore, in the ribs.

Daniel slipped into Portuguese, "Are you bankers?"

The two giant Americans looked at each other and laughed. They towered over him like the tops of question marks.

"I like these guys," Daniel thought.

Ladies in flowered muumuus with crying children on their laps were squeezed together on the seats. An assortment of bankers, businessmen, school children, and teenagers swayed together in the aisle.

Before Daniel knew what had happened, Elder Ron Chatfield and Elder Michael Moore had taught him the first missionary discussion right there on the bus, with hands hanging casually on the overhead bar. They took his address, but he wasn't really interested in talking to them about the gospel. He wanted to hear about the beautiful girls in California, about surfing in the ocean, and about skiing in the mountains.

Daniel saw the two missionaries again on the same bus route a month later. He motioned for them to sit by him and asked them why they hadn't visited him.

"We have been very busy," Elder Moore explained, and he promised they would drop by. *"Ciao,"* they said when they got off.

"Ciao," Daniel replied in parting.

"Two Americans came to the door today to talk to you, Daniel," his mother later told him as she sat on the couch, embroidering.

"Who? How do you know they were Americans?"

"They were tall, one like a giant, and I couldn't understand them. They talked like parrots."

Daniel laughed, quite sure the visitors had been the missionaries on the bus.

Daniel enjoyed the friendship of missionaries. Many came to his small home where Daniel invited other friends to listen to the message. He grew particularly fond of Elder Todd Andersen from Memphis, Tennessee, who entertained Daniel with stories of Elvis Presley and who also encouraged him with great love and patience.

Sometimes Daniel read parts of the Book of Mormon, but when he felt the warm flutter in his chest, he shut the book and often even ducked out the back door later to avoid the missionaries. He didn't want to get any closer to this fire, this burning in his chest. He liked to party and have a good time.

"Why haven't you been baptized yet?" The elders asked him a year later. Daniel didn't know why not. He had prayed and received answers to prayers and knew that the restored gospel was true. His mind wrestled with the problem, especially because he liked to please people and make them happy.

In the night Daniel dreamed a strange dream. He was standing near a pool in a suit, of all things. He felt a strange desire to jump in the pool, but at the same time he didn't want to, and he had awakened with a troubled mind, wondering how he should interpret the dream. Several nights later he dreamed he was being immersed in water, and he awoke, flailing his arms in the air and sputtering.

A few nights after that he dreamed he saw two men in white shirts on a bus. They were traveling to the beach to baptize people he knew. Daniel had a desire to be baptized too, but as he ran to get on the bus, it zoomed past him, leaving him standing in swirls of dust. Then he dreamed of a blond American who pointed to a mountain and said, "Now you have to climb it." He awoke in a cold sweat, his heart thumping, as he remembered the two blond missionaries who had first told him of the Church.

During this time his mother suddenly went to the hospital, diagnosed with cancer of the stomach. First he had lost his father. Now would his mother follow? What would Vivi, Rafael, and Gorda do without her? Of course, he would have to take care of them.

Early in the morning, he dragged down his street past the Ipiranga River. He walked over the rope bridge and stood in the center, swaying over the morning suds that swished into the river from kitchen drains. He thought upon the strange dreams and his mother's sickness, and all of this troubled him.

Daniel careened off the rope bridge and wound his way back to his small cement house. He paused in the kitchen and ran his fingers over his mother's black pot.

"I'm about to get scorched," he thought. His chest

burned as he kneeled beside his bed. "I'm sorry I've been so dumb. Please help my mother get better . . . and . . . and then I'll get baptized." As soon as he said it, he felt relieved.

His mother amazed the doctors when she suddenly, miraculously recovered, but it didn't amaze Daniel, who had expected it. She returned from the hospital a week later, and Daniel was baptized shortly after, on June 10.

Afterward, Daniel threw his arms around his mother, Vivi, Rafael, and Gorda. "Before, my life was very shallow and filled with activities that weren't important, but now I feel such peace and joy." He talked to them about the gospel, encouraging his mother and Vivi to learn more, and Daniel achieved what the missionaries call a "white Christmas" when they were baptized that December.

Daniel worked every Saturday with the missionaries, helping them hunt for and teach investigators. He loved missionary work, and the missionaries gave him their shirts, ties, and pants as they left for home. "For *your* mission," they said.

Daniel worked with inactive members and, because the Church taught him to be industrious, helped other youth find jobs. Within four months, he was called to be a counselor in the Sunday School presidency and soon afterward was made president of that organization.

"Mother, I want to go on a mission," Daniel said one Sunday afternoon. "Soon I will have been a member for one year, and I can go." He put his arm around her as they strolled along their street.

"Daniel, you haven't finished college yet. You must do this first." A cluster of tanned children tore between them, chasing a rag soccer ball.

"Mother, there are many missionaries who have not yet finished school."

"If you go first, you might never finish your education.

You will never understand enough to do something . . . big." She gestured outward with her hands.

"My mother," he said, facing her and gently lifting her chin. "You can count the seeds in an apple, but you can't ever count the apples in a seed."

They stood in the middle of the street and hugged while the Ipiranga River swished by with its morning suds. "You may go, my son," his mother said, "because a mission is also a big thing to do."

POSTSCRIPT: Daniel served in the Brazil Porto Alegre Mission.

Maly Souvanthong in refugee camp

Maly at age eighteen

ESCAPE FROM LAOS

PARENTS

Monh and Noutay Souvanthong

LOCATION OF STORY

Laos and Massachusetts

Six-year-old Maly watched her mother use a woven basket to scoop catfish out of the shallow Nong Seng River, in Laos, then hoist the basket on her hip and head toward their one-room wooden house along the shore.

Maly twirled, caught air in her billowing sarong, and danced beside the rice fields behind her mother. Her father was a fine carpenter. He had made their new wooden house after the water and wind had blown the old house down in a big storm.

She stooped and gathered her cloth doll into her arms. She had made it herself out of rags and had tied the neck with a string. She was a good builder too.

Maly's brother, Keo, who was one year older and wiser, grabbed her arm and pulled her behind a cluster of mango trees. He put his hand over her mouth. "Watch," he whispered.

Maly saw the pillow of dust plumping in the distance, then heard the rumble as three big trucks full of soldiers ground by, the huge tires spitting rocks and dirt.

"That's the third time I have seen these today," Keo spoke proudly. "Now, follow me." They scooted across the hills, past the jail where people were thrown if they disobeyed, and wiggled under a sun-bleached fence, then another. At the crest of a hill, Keo pushed her down flat on the dirt and pointed. They lay on their stomachs and watched the scene developing below.

Maly saw a man, his shirt ripped and hanging from his back, and a soldier shouting at him. The soldier shoved the man with the end of his gun and tied him to a tree. The man struggled against the ropes as the soldier raised his rifle.

Maly covered her mouth, jumped up, and ran with Keo right behind her—under the fences, up the hill. A shot punctured the air, and Maly squealed.

Later, after they had returned home, she heard her father's voice in the wooden house with her mother. "They said he stole something, but he did not. They just used him to set an example."

"I see," said her mother. "So they shot him like the others."

Her father continued, "In the village they line up a lot of men and shoot them, then throw their bodies in the Mekong, so anybody who tries to escape the Communists may see what happens. There are rumors." He lowered his voice. "It is time to go, I think."

"Time to go where?" Maly said softly, and for some reason, she shuddered.

In the early evening when the sun hung low in the horizon, her mother bathed Maly with two buckets of well water in front of the wooden house, and the sun steamed her body dry.

Soon after, her father told her, her brothers, and her sisters that they were ready to go on a big trip to France to see relatives. Maly jumped and clapped her hands. She watched her mother hurriedly pick up baby Mei and grab the three- and four-year-olds, Mani and Chan, by the hand. Keo was already outside with his father. When her mother told Maly to hurry, she started to run to fetch her rag doll and her jumping rope made of elastic bands.

"No, no! You don't need anything else. I have packed." Her mother pushed her toward the bicycle where her father was waiting.

Maly clutched the bottom of her sarong. Her father hoisted her onto the platform he had built on the bicycle, where she would sit with her two sisters. She searched her father's face, and although he smiled, she could see that behind his smile was a wooden face. Maly rolled her fists and rubbed tears from her eyes.

She watched her mother climb on a friend's motorcycle with the two boys, and Maly reached her arms toward her and cried, "Ma, ma, ma."

"Hush, sweet one. You must learn to be quiet," her father's steely voice commanded. "You will cause the others to cry."

She choked on his unusual harshness and blinked back her tears.

They rode to the house of her parents' friend, where they stayed until two in the morning. Maly slept on the floor and later felt her father lift her in the ebony of night.

She heard her father whisper to her mother as their feet shuffled quietly on the soft dirt. "My youngest brother was caught. They shaved his head and took him to jail.

"Ttttttt. That is bad. It is right that we left when we did."

"See, there is only a piece of the moon. It is a blessing."

"We must keep the children quiet."

Her father and a strange man slid a canoe into the Mekong River. Maly climbed in silently, while her sleeping sisters were lifted in.

"Hush," the canoe man murmured. "No one must speak. Be still as a shrine." The canoe sliced into the water without a splash.

"Duck down. Don't move."

Maly felt her mother's hand pressing down upon her head, and she started to whimper because she wanted her doll and her rope.

Her mother whispered, "You must not make noise, or we will all get caught and die."

Maly covered her mouth with her hands. She pressed hard and swallowed a choke so they would not die.

A spotlight from a lighthouse swept across the water—searching, probing. She heard her mother stop breathing as the light brushed the tip of the canoe and then swept beyond.

They continued on: paddle—duck down—pause. The light stopped a few feet from the canoe like a bloodhound tracking a scent. Maly hiccoughed. She sucked in her lips, bit down, and tasted blood as the spotlight swung ahead again. They slid a few yards at a time, then a little further.

After thirty minutes, they tiptoed out of the canoe onto Thailand soil.

Her mother's arms held her sisters, and her father's arms held Chan. Maly clutched her sarong and sucked on a wadded corner. Keo copied her father's gait and tried to act like a man, while her father paced like a caged panther along the shore of the river. "Where is that boy who was supposed to meet us?" he whispered. "Where is he? It will soon be light."

Then a boy who appeared to be fishing in the sliver of the moon's reflection motioned to them. "Follow me," he said.

As the boy led them into a barn, her father breathed a deep breath. Maly wiggled down into the hay and slept.

She awakened several times to see her father sitting cross-legged, his body silhouetted against the faint light from the window. He spoke softly in a strained voice with the boy's parents, planning what to do from there.

The next morning her mother shook her shoulders, then gave her a bowl of rice and some dried fish. Maly held Mani's hand as they walked along the dirt road through a Thai village lined with thatched roofs slung over wooden huts.

"Where are we going?" Maly asked.

"I want to go home," Mani whimpered.

A policeman walked toward them, and Maly looked up at her father. His face looked calm, but she heard him suck in his breath and saw his arms tighten around Chan. The policeman stopped them and said some things Maly didn't understand. Her heart raced like the clouds in a storm.

The policeman took them to something that looked to Maly like a round lighthouse with bars on the windows. At least seventy people were crammed inside. There was only one small bathroom and a shower. Babies cried, while wrinkled and bent people lay on the floor, panting and wiping sweat from their foreheads.

Maly watched her mother reach through the bars to offer money to a man driving by in a cart, selling bananas and fresh mangoes. She slept on the cement floor with her head in her mother's lap, too tired to feel the hardness. In the evening soldiers brought them squash, pumpkins, and water.

They stayed two days at the first facility in the fall before a truck drove them to a refugee camp. Maly noticed a tall cement wall with barbed wire laced along the top, which surrounded their new quarters. Small, wooden houses were scattered across the dirt inside the wall. One long tub, the length of a large truck, sat near the middle of the compound, and everyone used the water for both drinking and washing. There were no trees, only the open field and the surrounding wall.

Maly's family was assigned to a long wooden house where about two hundred people were sandwiched together, with mosquito netting separating them into three sections. There was an outhouse with ten toilets outside the building, which Maly hated to visit because the odor made her stomach twist.

There were no sinks, no appliances. Each person was required to have a bowl in order to be fed their two meals a day, usually a thin soup; but since Maly was a child, she sometimes received sweet milk and bananas also.

"Why do they keep us in jails?" Maly soon asked her father.

"Because the Thai people do not want us to mix with them. They do not want us to stay in their country, because it is not ours." Her father paced and squeezed his hands and then picked her up in his arms. "There is a place that will accept us. They take everybody, even old people. It is far away, and it is America." He smiled, and Maly saw the muscles in his neck relax.

"When can we go?"

"We must wait our turn."

Soon Maly's stomach stopped clawing at her like an angry tiger, even though the bone bumped out on her wrist. She and Keo passed the hot, muggy days digging holes in the dirt and shooting pebbles into them.

She saw that people who had no families were ignored, and some of them died.

"Family is everything. You must always be with a family," her father coached her. "Families protect each other."

In one camp, a man tried to escape. When the police caught him, they told the other refugees to go inside their shelters and shut the doors and shutters on the glassless windows.

Maly heard the slash of sticks and the escapee yelling and screaming. Curious, she creaked the wooden window open a few inches to watch.

The escapee lay on the ground with his legs drawn to his chest. Several policemen were beating upon him with bamboo sticks. They left him groaning on the ground with blood streaked over his face and torn clothes.

Maly's mother snatched her by the arm away from the window and squeezed her. Then Maly held her stomach and crouched behind her mother. She always stayed as far away from the guards as possible after that and covered her mouth when they stamped by in heavy boots.

Eleven months after escaping across the Mekong River, Maly and her family boarded a plane to leave Thailand. To Maly it was like crawling into the jaws of a huge dragon. She clung to her mother's sarong and longed to go back to the little wooden house her father had built, nestled beside the Nong Seng River. She wished to run through rice fields, to eat mangoes and fresh fish from her mother's basket, to hold her doll and jump with her rope, but she didn't cry so they would not die.

When Maly went into the bathroom at the back of the plane, the room was tiny, so she went in alone. She sucked in her breath and held her mouth because another girl was in there, and she was holding her mouth too. The girl copied everything she did. Maly reached out and was surprised to touch a hard surface. Was the girl trapped inside that shiny place? Maly dove backward out of the bathroom, pointing.

A woman told her, "That is a mirror, and that is you in the mirror. It is a reflection, like looking into the mighty Mekong."

On a white screen in the plane, people spoke and moved as if they were alive, but they were only flat, moving pictures of them.

More surprises awaited Maly when they landed in Salem, Massachusetts. An uncle and his sponsor picked them up at the airport. The buildings were taller than trees, and thousands of houses were scattered everywhere with smooth roads running between, filled with speeding cars of every shape and color.

A Christian church gave them more clothes than Maly had ever seen, but she didn't like to crowd her feet into shoes all the time. The Christian church taught her about a new God who was different from Buddha, and she and her brothers and sisters began to learn English at the elementary school they attended. When snow fell, she ran outside and wondered who was spilling this cold, wet stuff over the houses.

Her father found work as a carpenter, and her mother worked at a shoe factory and also made clothes for people. She and her family lived in Salem for four years before they moved to Lynn, Massachusetts.

Maly's brother Keo was the first member of the family to encounter the Mormon church. The missionaries found him when he was sixteen and Maly was fifteen. He attended church secretly at first and was also the first in the family to be baptized.

One evening in May, after Maly had showered and snuggled down in Mani and Mei's bedroom to watch television, the missionaries knocked on their door. "Keo isn't home," Mei answered.

The missionaries invited all the family members to the living room to discuss the gospel. Maly hid in the bedroom. Mei and Mani came in, tugged on Maly's arm, and said, "They won't talk to us if you're not there, too. Please come."

Maly joined her mother and sisters in the living room. A Laotian, Elder Vang, translated for her mother, and Elder Easton gave Maly a copy of the Book of Mormon. He circled some verses and told them all to pray to find out if the message were true.

Maly was a little confused, but then she thought, "Maybe he's telling us something true. These boys have strong beliefs, and I can give it a try." So she read, prayed, and was amazed at her feelings. She shared her experience with Mani. "I felt different. I felt a peace and something warm that I had never felt before. I'm excited to learn more."

Maly began attending church, but her parents were not interested. They preferred to follow Buddha as their ancestors had before them, but they told Maly, her sisters, and brother that the Mormon church taught them good things, and they allowed them to attend.

One Sunday a young girl bore her testimony, and as she shared precious thoughts, Maly felt the spirit of the girl's words. When she arrived back home, she called the missionaries on the phone and told them she wanted to be baptized, like her brother Keo.

In June, just one month after Maly listened to the first missionary lesson, she and her sisters were baptized by Elders Easton and Vang. Keo stood with arms folded over his chest, his eyes shining as he watched.

Maly grew enthusiastic to share the gospel with two cousins who had just moved from Laos. She helped translate for the missionaries, and her cousins joined the church too. Later, she shared the gospel with two other cousins from West Virginia, and they also joined the Church.

At youth dances, she grabbed shy boys and girls, hiding in shadows against the walls, and pulled them into the center of the floor to dance. Her cheerful laughter and

disarming smile thawed the fears of the most timid
youths. She gathered everyone together at activities—
Anglos, Asians, nonmembers—whoever would come.

She qualified for the basketball team at high school,
sang in the school chorus, played tennis, and worked hard
for good grades. She volunteered at Union Hospital, and
she served dinners for the homeless on holidays. She also
conducted music in sacrament meeting, read in the Book
of Mormon, prayed, and felt her spirit swell.

However, in the summer, friends tried to entice her
away from the Church. "Why do you go to church and
waste your time?"

Another friend asked, "Why do you believe this stuff?"

At the same time, her parents and relatives pressed
her. "You are becoming an Anglo, but you are Asian. You
must not forget who you are. Remember Laos."

"Family is everything, and you must obey your elders."

Maly sat on her bed and looked at a photograph of the
Washington Temple on one wall and the drawing of
Buddha on the other wall. She rolled her hands into fists
and rubbed tears from her eyes. What should she do? Who
was right? She felt trapped and wondered what it would
feel like if she left the Church?

Maly was magnetically pulled to her friends, but she
felt as if her feet were slipping on pebbles. She stopped
attending church. A month passed while she vacillated
between her friends' coaxing smiles and the concerned
looks of Mormon youth leaders.

Her Young Women leader, Sister Louise La Count, visited her and counseled her repeatedly. "Pray, Maly," she
said. "Don't be afraid to ask."

Maly pulled her patriarchal blessing from her dresser
drawer. She read that stumbling blocks would come to
her, but that she must turn those stumbling blocks into
stepping stones. Then she steeled herself to accept the

answer and prayed. She received the same warm feeling that had become so comforting and familiar, and she knew what she must do.

"I must go to church again," she told Sister La Count.

"You have made the right decision."

"But I feel so guilty. Will God ever forgive me?" Tigers still slashed about in her head. God had led her all the way from Laos to a land of freedom where she could learn of Heavenly Father, and she had thrown this precious knowledge into the trash can.

She accepted a call to serve a mini-mission for youth to the Arlington Ward. As she sat with the sister missionaries on the carpet of their small apartment, circling important verses in sixty copies of the Book of Mormon, the rain slashed against the window.

She asked the sisters, "Can Heavenly Father really forgive? Let's say the person rejected him. How can she get forgiveness when she can't forgive herself?" Maly covered the tears in her eyes.

One sister read, "Though your sins be as scarlet, they shall be as white as snow; though they be red like crimson, they shall be as wool." (Isaiah 1:18.) The missionaries took her to her bishop, Paul Dredge. He counseled her that what she was experiencing was part of growing up, and he gave her a priesthood blessing. Maly felt the tigers fleeing as he placed his hands upon her head. She felt her body being washed in brightness, her spirit in forgiveness, and she understood.

"Everyone makes mistakes," she said. "I understand now that God forgives us, but we must forgive ourselves. I believe that the reason he sent me to Arlington on this mini-mission was to face my own problems and to let me know he forgives me and cares, but I will not fall away from God again. I will listen with my heart."

She was called to be a counselor in the Young Women

organization and asked to be a junior counselor at girls' camp. She attended seminary and also awakened her younger sisters each Sunday, played church tapes for them in the morning, and herded them into the church. "You must remember," she told them, "that the Holy Ghost helps us to know the truth; but we must work to have it with us, so that is why you must get up and go to church."

She began speaking at baptisms, which occurred almost weekly in their Asian branch. She often spoke about the Holy Ghost and adversity. "The Holy Ghost tells us the truth of all things," she explained. "It comforts us. It can make us feel better when we are sad or worried. It can warn us of danger . . . God always loves us no matter what we do, but we must ask him for help and turn to him if we want help.

"I have learned that I could escape from the fear of camps, of shootings, of losing my home, but the biggest trial of all is facing the fears in my own mind. My Asian culture is part of the blood that flows in me, and I will never reject that. But far from the banks of the Nong Seng River, I have had to blend that wisdom with my new heritage, a peaceful, lasting heritage as a daughter of God."

POSTSCRIPT: Maly was called to be Young Women president in the Asian branch at age eighteen.

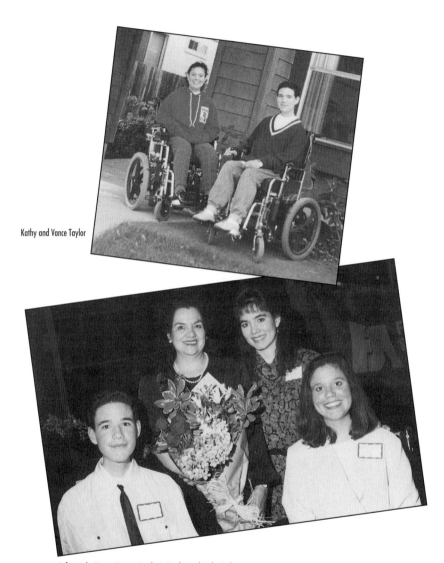

Kathy and Vance Taylor

Left to right: Vance, Morena (mother), Martha, and Kathy Taylor

"A SPECIAL KIND OF COURAGE"

PARENTS

Morena and Bill Taylor

LOCATION OF STORY

Petaluma, California

Seven-year-old Vance Taylor chased his sister Kathy across the lawn in front of their Victorian home in Humboldt, California. Kathy stumbled and rolled on the grass. Vance grabbed his sister's hand and pulled her up, then charged toward the mulberry tree.

"Can't catch me, Kathy," he yelled over his shoulder.

Kathy trailed behind him, so Vance slowed down, skipping just out of her reach. Pouncing forward, his sister grabbed his shirt, stumbled again, pulled him down, and they giggled and wrestled on the prickly grass.

Later Vance shopped at the Safeway store with his mother and two sisters, Kathy, nine, and Martha, twelve. Kathy complained, "I can't hold the milk. It's too heavy. I'm going to drop it."

Martha, who was pushing the grocery cart, reached for the milk. "I can take it."

Vance raised his chin and flexed his biceps. "No, let me. I can carry it for you," he reassured Kathy. He knew he could carry the sacks, climb over fences, and run faster than she.

When they arrived home, Vance grabbed Kathy's hand. "Come on, Kathy, let's go play tag. You're 'it.'"

Kathy flopped down on the love seat in the living room and said, "I don't want to."

Vance begged, "You don't have to be 'it.' I'll be 'it.' Come on."

"I'm too tired," Kathy complained.

Puzzled, Vance watched his sister curl up in a little ball, nestled in the crook of the couch arm. "How come she's always tired?" he asked his mother.

"Maybe she just didn't get enough sleep."

"But she's always too tired."

He saw lines wrinkle between his mother's eyes and knew it meant she was worried.

When Kathy began to walk with hunched shoulders, her legs thrown out to her sides, Vance's mother took his sister to a medical clinic in Santa Rosa, where the doctor ordered blood tests and other lab work.

When the results of the tests arrived, Vance asked his mother about them.

"They show that Kathy has high levels of a chemical called CPK," she answered.

"What does that mean?"

"I'm not sure, but the doctor didn't really act concerned. She might outgrow it."

Several months later, they stopped at a brand-new Burger King for hamburgers. Vance scampered in front to grab a place in the line, where twenty people were already waiting to be served. A young employee taking orders pointed at Kathy, hobbling forward with little thrusts. It seemed to Vance that all twenty people whirled around to stare at his sister, and a boy in the line jabbed his friend in the ribs and snickered.

Vance's throat swelled as he looked back at Kathy, and suddenly he hated these people and wanted to throw his shirt over his sister's face.

Kathy whispered, "I can't do this. I'm going to cry."

Their mother answered calmly, "No, you mustn't cry. Stare them right in the face and smile. Just remember the doctor thinks you might outgrow this."

Vance watched Kathy force a radiant smile through her clouded eyes.

Some people looked down while others looked the other way. After the Taylors left, Vance's mother hugged Kathy and spoke to him and Martha. "You have just witnessed courage of the highest kind."

Over the next two years, Vance started stumbling too, and he wondered why he fell more often than his friends. He pushed harder to scramble over fences and began walking with a shuffle, lifting his heel with a little forward thrust. He climbed stairs by lifting his right leg first.

"Are you trying to copy Kathy's walk?" his mother asked Vance.

Vance looked down and shook his head. Was he catching the same thing his sister had?

"Regardless of how unconcerned the doctor feels, I'm taking you two to a specialist."

Vance and Kathy went with their mother to a neurologist at the University of California Medical Center in San Francisco. The doctor performed a biopsy, cutting a small sample of the thigh muscle tissue from each child to send to the lab for analysis.

On Thanksgiving day, the phone rang. His mother answered it, and Vance watched as her face turned white. She hung up, and as she sat back down at the table, she smiled. But the smile looked forced to Vance. "That was the results of the lab tests on both of you," she said.

His father stopped chewing and looked up. Vance could sense the tension between his parents. They were trying to hide it from the children, but he knew his mom and dad weren't getting along very well.

His mother looked down and said, "Well, everything is going to be okay. The children are going to be fine." She smiled at him, then at Kathy.

"Is that all?" his father asked.

"Well, there is one little problem," his mother added. "The children should know it too, but it's something we can live with."

Vance watched his father's eyebrows pull together.

"The children have something called muscular dystrophy."

His dad dropped his fork. It clattered against the plate and dropped to the floor. His dad leaned down to get it, and when he straightened up, his face was red, and he wouldn't look at anyone.

"What's mus . . . cu . . . lar, whatever you said?" Martha asked.

Vance watched his mother, looking for clues in her face. She looked nervously at his father and then turned to the children. "Muscular dystrophy is a disease of the muscles. That's why you have been stumbling, but you'll be okay." She smiled at them, and Vance believed her.

"Some kids make fun of me at school. They think I'm retarded." Kathy covered her face with her hands. "Would you still love me if I was retarded or handicapped?" Kathy asked.

His mother got up from the table, walked around and hugged Kathy. "Of course, I would. I always will, no matter what."

"And me too," Martha grabbed Kathy's hands.

His father leaned over and kissed her forehead.

Vance looked at his sister and smiled. "You're probably

my best friend," Vance said, reassuring his sister and himself too.

Kathy's dimples puckered at the sides of a broad smile.

Vance watched his sister with more interest now. Would the same things happen to him too? Would he continue to lose more of his strength. He later stared at the full-length mirror to see if he could see any changes. He had the same brown, wavy hair, and he looked just as tall and slim, but inside a harsh sandpaper feeling rubbed against his chest. He was different. Something was happening to the muscles in his legs, and he knew it. Why was God letting this happen to him—to both of them?

In January, during a hospital checkup in San Francisco, Vance learned that muscular dystrophy is a crippling disease that attacks all the muscles in the body. Vance looked at Kathy to see her reaction, and she smiled at him. He still wasn't quite sure what the disease would mean to him, but if Kathy could still smile, he could too.

When he returned home, he was startled to see his father's suitcase and briefcase sitting by the door, and after listening to his parents argue, he learned that his father and mother were separating.

"Why is he doing this?" Kathy covered her face. "He's walking out on all of us, and it's my fault."

"I'm not walking out on you," he reassured her and squeezed her shoulders. "You must understand that we have other reasons."

As his father left, Vance sniffed back tears and hugged his sister. His mom pulled all three children close. "It's not your fault. But we can help each other, and don't worry, I'll never leave you. We're in this together."

"I can help both of you," Martha choked, "and you too, Mom."

Later when he was alone, Vance cried into his pillow.

Why was God allowing all this to happen to him? He prayed for help, for understanding, and for strength. At length his tears dried, leaving cool tracks on his cheeks. A gentle peace settled over him, but he felt very weak and tired when he finally fell asleep.

One crisp spring morning, Vance sat in the back seat of their Astro Van with a head cold. Martha had left earlier to school for a meeting, and he watched his sister Kathy as she got out of the car to go into the elementary school. She slowly hobbled over to the gutter, then struggled to lift her leg on the curb. Her brown curls tumbled over her shoulders as she leaned forward.

"Such effort for such a small thing." His mother dabbed her eyes with a tissue.

Pushing against the hood of an old blue Chevy, Kathy flung her weight up onto her foot and finally pushed herself up over the curb. Then she turned with an Olympic-medal smile and waved good-bye.

His mother squeezed his hands in hers. "Today, Vance, I sat here crying as I watched my daughter fighting to do something so simple, but she just taught me a lesson. Instead of being sad, I should be happy that although she had to struggle, today she could do it herself."

Vance's eyes grew large and round as he looked at his mother.

Kathy tried out her first scooter wheelchair when she was thirteen. Sometimes when Kathy tried to climb into her wheelchair, Vance, who could still walk, stood behind her and held the chair so it wouldn't slip. By sixth grade Vance needed a wheelchair too, but it was okay, because Kathy could do most everything from hers.

Vance decided he wanted to play the drums at school, and he was one of three children selected for that position.

He tapped out rhythmic beats, his fingers a blur, and the doctor wondered how he could move his hands so quickly.

One spring day Vance's schoolteacher, Mr. Dwelley, announced, "We're going to go on a three-day field trip into Wolf Creek."

Students cheered and banged fists on their desks. But Vance looked down at his wheelchair and wondered how he could possibly go, and he had to admit to himself that he couldn't do as much as other kids.

Mr. Dwelley walked up to Vance and rested a hand on his shoulder. "I want you to come too, Vance. We can manage with your wheelchair."

Vance beamed.

Unfortunately, after Vance's mother had dropped him off for the three-day field trip, his wheelchair broke down during the first hour of rugged trail bumps. He looked around at everyone and felt heat rise up his neck. What would he do now?

A ranger came along, and Mr. Dwelley asked, "Would you cart this wheelchair back to the lodge? This young man is coming with us."

Mr. Dwelley hoisted Vance on his shoulders and carried him around the fishery. "Look, Vance, you can see the salmon spawning."

"I can carry Vance's pack," one friend offered.

Another added, "And I can carry his sleeping bag."

When Mr. Dwelley grew tired, other parents took shifts carrying Vance on their backs as they hiked through giant redwoods.

They stopped in front of the tallest tree that Vance had ever seen, and although Vance towered above all his friends on Mr. Dwelley's shoulders, he felt like a flea compared to the tree. "See this tree, Vance?" Mr. Dwelley said. "This is the tallest redwood in the United States. It's about two hundred feet high. Lightning struck it once, but you know something? It's such a strong tree, that it didn't even lose any branches. It just sort of said, 'Go ahead, lightning. Hit me. See if I care.'" Mr. Dwelley turned his head up, and Vance could see him smile.

Vance thought about that. He liked that tough tree that wouldn't lose its branches. It looked to Vance as if he could climb right off the top branches into the stars, and he wondered if God lived up there. Could Vance touch him? Could God work a miracle for him?

At the end of camp, when Vance returned on Mr. Dwelley's shoulders, his enthusiasm spilled out in a waterfall of words. "Mom, I had the best time of my life. I saw bears, and one pounded right on the window in the lodge and almost broke through." Mr. Dwelley lifted Vance into his wheelchair.

His mother buried her head in her son's tangled hair. "You smell like a bonfire," she said, laughing.

"And I saw squirrels and lots of birds, and guess what else?" His tanned face flushed as he smiled up at his teacher. "I had the best seat in the whole house."

His mother reached into her vinyl bag for a handkerchief, then grabbed Mr. Dwelley's hand.

"It was nothing," he said. "Five years ago, I was diagnosed with cancer. This year my cancer came back, and I was told it was terminal. I felt no more purpose in living until Vance came into my classroom. Everytime there was a task, he would smile a big, broad grin and find a way to do it. He gave me the courage I needed to continue going. So you see, Mrs. Taylor, I'm the one who is grateful."

When Vance was twelve, he, his mother, and sisters moved to Petaluma, California. Martha grew interested in the Church when a girlfriend invited her to attend a sacrament meeting. She started receiving missionary lessons secretly, then finally invited them to her home.

Vance and Kathy wheeled into the family room for one of Martha's missionary discussions. The missionaries included both Vance and Kathy in a lively conversation. At the end of the lesson, Elder Christopher Monson said, "Maybe you two can get some of these lessons sometime." He nodded at Vance and Kathy.

"Oh, really?" Vance wheeled closer over the flat carpet and looked up at Elder Monson. "Well, how much does it cost?"

The missionaries smiled, and Elder Lance Smith said, "They're free."

"Whoa," Vance replied. "Free?"

When the missionaries left, Vance said, "It feels like they took something with them. The shine that was in here just disappeared."

Martha was baptized that spring, in April. Vance and Kathy continued attending church with her, while his mother usually drove them there.

When the missionaries challenged them to pray to find out if the Church were true, Vance decided to try it. Peace slowly blanketed him that evening, and the following morning he told his mother softly, "I prayed last night, and Heavenly Father told me that this church is true." He and Kathy were baptized together on May 27, and their mother joined them in August.

When Vance was fourteen, the doctor announced some frightening news: "Vance, you are going to have to undergo some rather serious surgery."

"Surgery?" Vance asked nervously.

"Yes. Your back is buckling down, and as a result, it's squeezing your heart and lungs. Without surgery you eventually won't be able to breathe, and your heart won't be able to function, either."

Vance felt numb. "Can't you do something else?"

"What kind of surgery do you mean?" his mother asked.

"I would have to implant two steel rods in Vance's back, anchoring them to his spine and to his hip," he explained, motioning with his hands.

"I'm scared. I don't want this surgery," Vance pleaded.

"I have to warn you," the doctor continued, turning to Vance's mother, "this procedure could cause him to lose the already-limited use of his hands and his arms." He paused. "He won't be able to feed himself anymore. In addition, he won't be able to bend forward or backward after the surgery. Even with the surgery, we can correct his posture by only sixty percent."

His mother put her hands over her face.

"There's just one more thing. He will experience a great deal of pain."

"I don't want any surgery," Vance protested. "Couldn't you have done something before I got this bad?"

In the evening Vance cried, "Why would Heavenly Father do something like this to me?"

His mother hugged him. "Maybe he didn't *do* this to you. Maybe there's some other reason for it."

Vance choked. "I know. I keep remembering Jesus saying, 'Thy will be done.' I know that whatever is happening is more than I can see."

At the same time Vance, his mother, and both sisters were invited to attend Especially for Youth, a Church program in Provo, Utah, that develops spirituality and leadership in youth. Vance really wanted to attend because he felt it might help to give him the strength he needed to face his surgery.

Going to EFY was a great opportunity for them, but it presented a financial problem. His mother worked at Sonoma State University and had a bachelor's degree in management and psychology, but she still had to struggle to raise her three children by herself and to pay all their medical bills. In spite of the difficulties, they packed their bags and prayed that somehow they would be able to go to EFY before Vance's scheduled surgery. Two days before they were to leave, they received anonymous donations from the stake, sufficient to fund their trip.

On the morning that Brad Wilcox, a noted youth speaker and friend of the Taylor family, was scheduled to speak to all the youth at BYU, the Taylors arrived one hour early at the Wilkinson Center so that they could have front row seats.

When Brad rose to speak, he said, "I want to introduce you to three friends of mine." He asked Martha to stand, and everyone clapped. "She's great," he said, "but she's just the first one."

"Oh, no," Vance thought, "he's going to embarrass us and say our names in front of everyone."

"There are two more to go," Brad continued. "These next two won't stand up, because they can't. They are in wheelchairs." He asked Vance and Kathy to wheel up and down the rows and smile and wave at the other young people, and everyone applauded again.

"They both have muscular dystrophy. Now, Vance is scheduled for some very serious surgery in a few days, and the doctors aren't too optimistic. They think that Vance won't be able to move his hands anymore and that he'll lose whatever strength he has left, but there's one thing the doctors didn't count on. They didn't count on you young people and your prayers. Vance needs your prayers now, and he needs you to fast and pray for him by name."

Then he added, "All of you, when you're feeling down and you think you can't keep on going, I want you to remember Vance and Kathy Taylor." The entire audience stood up and cheered with the same fervor as if they were at the Super Bowl.

Vance wiped his sleeve over his eyes, and he reached out and squeezed Kathy's hand.

"And Vance and Kathy, when you feel that you can't go on, that it's too difficult, I want you to remember these one thousand young people cheering for you."

The youth continued to cheer. Later, they fasted, and at every devotional they prayed for Kathy and Vance. Vance fasted too for all the other youth to have the strength to keep fasting.

Vance wanted a priesthood blessing, and that same week a friend drove Vance and his family to Salt Lake City to see Elder Robert E. Wells of the First Quorum of the Seventy. Elder Wells placed his hands on Vance's head and promised him that he would have the best doctor available to perform the surgery.

Vance knew he already had a doctor scheduled to operate in September, and he wasn't known as one of the best, but he thought, "I'll just wait and see."

Then Elder Wells also promised him that his recovery would be considered a miracle among the medical community, that he would have little pain, and that his recovery would be fast. Vance felt the power of that special blessing.

The family returned to California, their spiritual batteries recharged with new faith and hope. On the following Thursday, the previously scheduled doctor called to apologize. He told Vance's mother that he wouldn't be able to do the surgery on Vance because the insurance wouldn't pay for it. Instead, he suggested a Dr. David Bradford, who had performed hundreds of such surgeries.

After some research, Vance's mother learned that Dr. Bradford was considered the best spinal surgeon on the West coast and perhaps the best in the country. When she shared the news with Vance, he remembered the blessing and smiled at his mother.

However, Dr. Bradford was booked through November, but if they waited for the surgery until after November, it would interfere with Martha's upcoming wedding to Christopher Monson, the missionary who had baptized her and Vance.

When Dr. Bradford heard of the conflict, he opened his schedule for them, and on September 11, Dr. Bradford spent eight hours operating on Vance's back.

Vance's mother later told him that Dr. Bradford had looked exhausted after the surgery, but that he had walked into the waiting room and hugged her. He had said, "Everything went fine. Don't ask me how, but I got his posture corrected one hundred percent."

"We know how," Vance later told his mother, and she nodded.

Each day when the doctor checked under his bandages, he remarked about his rapid recovery. Vance simply looked at his mom and winked.

"Look, Mom!" Vance exclaimed after a week. "I can move my hands."

After four weeks, he surprised his mother again. "Watch what I can do now." He bent forward in the bed, then backward.

"Oh, doesn't that hurt, Vance?"

"Not much," he said, his face winced with determination.

Vance continued to astound everyone when, after six weeks, he could brush his own teeth and comb his hair.

Seven weeks following his surgery, Vance astonished everyone again by returning to school in his wheelchair. Later he asked his mom if she thought it would be possible for someone in a wheelchair to run for vice president of the sophomore class.

"Why not?" she answered. "You can do whatever you set your mind to."

So Vance ran for vice president, and in his campaign speech he said to the students, "I can't promise any miracles in this school, but who knows, maybe there will be a miracle or two along the way."

Vance won the school election, and he was also selected as president of the seminary student council and called to be president of his teachers quorum. He began receiving invitations to speak at ward and stake functions. In his speeches he encouraged others to try to achieve goals, stating such things as: "I decided to write a song dedicated to my mom, titled, 'A Special Kind of Courage.' My mom is the greatest lady. I thank God every day for giving her to me.

"And I want to write a book. I think everyone should have a dream. I want to go to BYU, major in public speaking and politics. That's the way it works. You dream a dream, fast and pray, and fulfill it. Once it's fulfilled, dream again. And along the way, who knows? Maybe another miracle or two will happen."

Audrey Chase. Below, she is with
Senator Orrin Hatch, lobbying
for a national tree fund.

PLANTING

PARENTS
Ronna and Kevin Chase

LOCATION OF STORY
Salt Lake City, Utah, and Menan, Idaho

Twelve-year-old Audrey Chase packed all her possessions into cardboard boxes in her home in Salt Lake
City. They lined her bedroom floor like brown boxcars in
a train, some without lids, some dented with masking
tape bandages. She heard her mother's voice, "Hurry,
Audrey. I need you to help me pack the dishes."

"I'll be there. I'm almost finished." Running out of
space, Audrey gathered an assortment of pencils, pastes,
erasers, paints, and charcoal in her arms, dumped them
into a plastic garbage sack, and placed them on top of the
last box. "This is the coal car," she said to herself. All her
life's work reduced to five boxes, each one carrying her
precious cargo, the proof that she had lived.

Anxiety pushed up her throat, but she swallowed it
down. She couldn't control the awful things happening to
her family, but organizing her possessions made her feel
in charge again, at least of part of her life.

"I know I couldn't make it without my Father in
Heaven," Audrey whispered. She was positive there would

be a divorce now. The Holy Ghost kept assuring her that it was not her fault. Since she had always been the leader of her younger sisters and brothers, she found it hard to believe that there was nothing she could have done to stop it.

She lingered in her bedroom, kneeled down on the rough carpet, and pulled the first box toward her. She needed to touch her awards from her tree projects, her picture in Congress, her journal, to reassure herself that they were all still there, that her life was marching forward like the cardboard train to some destination where everything would be okay again.

When had she first learned to rely on her Father in Heaven? she wondered, then remembered. In kindergarten she had been petrified that her dog, Sharmane, would die. She and her dad had played Frisbee with the black Doberman on the turf farm behind their old house. Audrey's younger sisters had all learned to walk by hanging onto Sharmane for balance. When Sharmane ripped her sides open on a wire fence, Audrey prayed, then she tugged on her dad's sleeve and begged, "Please give her a blessing, Dad." Her father hugged Audrey and gave Sharmane a blessing. The vet performed surgery, and Sharmane recovered, but more important, Audrey had learned to rely on her Father in Heaven.

Audrey had depended upon his strength again in another crisis when she was seven. Her family—Mom, Dad, her little sisters, Beverly, Carina, and Darlene—had driven to Menan, Idaho, to visit relatives. It was dark, and she had awakened to the voices of her mother and father arguing in the front seat of the station wagon.

She realized the car had broken down, and they were stranded. What could she do to solve the problem? She knew several friends whose parents had argued a lot and then divorced, and she began to cry into the checkered quilt wrapped around her, the quilt her great grandma had made.

Then Audrey prayed, "Please don't let my parents get a divorce." After she finished, her parents quit arguing, and she felt peaceful, knowing everything was calm again. Three hours later her grandparents found them at the side of the road and helped them.

Besides developing faith at an early age, Audrey knew she had also demonstrated leadership in her family by creating a basement school where she could teach her younger sisters and brothers. She lined them up, along with her dolls, and made them her first students. She not only taught her sisters and brothers to pray to Father in Heaven, but she also tried to teach them to read. Carina, who was quiet and four years younger, cooperated, and Audrey succeeded in teaching her to pray and read. When Erik and Gavin joined the family, the boys wouldn't stay in their seats at all, and Audrey discovered her first discipline problem.

She resolved the problem by telling stories. Audrey had learned the great magnetic pull of a good book. She gathered her brothers and sisters around her to teach them to read from the book *Hop on Pop,* which developed jam-smeared and tattered pages and had to be replaced three times. Audrey's cheeks flushed as Erik pointed at the words and repeated them. She knew then that when she grew up, she wanted to be a teacher.

Her strongest school leadership occurred at Jackson Elementary, a low-income and transient school, where she qualified for the special program for academically talented children. Audrey's faith and enthusiasm exploded in this class, where her teacher taught her to think and to solve real problems, just what Audrey had always loved to do with her family.

Audrey and the other students in her fourth-grade class decided the world needed more trees. They chose to adopt a park near their school and planned to plant at least a hundred trees there. But that took money, so the students wrote proposals for a city grant of money to purchase the trees.

Audrey prayed in her mind, "Please help me to do a good job writing this up." She had always relied on her Father in Heaven to help her before, and now she knew he could also help her to write a winning grant application. Audrey's proposal was chosen to submit to the city, which awarded the grant. Audrey had to sign a formal document to receive the $1,500 for the trees.

One day in class, Audrey's brain buzzed with ideas. "We ought to try to get money for other kids to plant trees too—all over Utah."

"Yeah. And let's be like a club." Josh's root beer-colored eyes widened.

A student suggested, "Let's call ourselves the Tree Club."

"No, 'Root for Trees' Club," someone else said. Everyone laughed.

"How about 'Trees Are Tree-mendous'?"

Audrey squinted one eye before adding, "How about, the 'Leaf It to Us' Club?"

The students chose Audrey's title, and she and her friends successfully lobbied the state legislature for two years, receiving $20,000 in a fund for students all over Utah to plant trees. The students elected Audrey as their president, partly because she never bragged.

Audrey slipped into leadership as naturally as she slipped on her red striped tights, which she loved to wear. Her grades soared to straight A's. She couldn't wait to get to school each day. Her activities kept her so busy that she did not notice her parents' lack of communication and frequent disagreements. Thinking about what she should be solving at home was hard when TV reporters interviewed her about the tree fund.

In fifth grade she received a great opportunity. Because of her leadership, a KSL television reporter asked her if she would like to write a five-minute Arbor Day news story on the importance of trees. Audrey could hardly believe it, but how could she do that? Of course, she knew. She prayed to Heavenly Father and then asked her teacher for advice and her mother to help. Audrey wrote the script, which was aired on Arbor Day in the spring. She beamed as she sat with her family watching the videotape.

Still caught up in school leadership, she had a more spectacular thought. She raised her hand in class, tossed her perfectly crimped hair, and said, "If we could get money like this in Utah for kids to plant trees, why don't we try to do it for the whole nation?"

"Like in Colorado, and New York, and even Alaska," Josh added.

Her teacher took three steps back, laughed, threw out her arms on either side, and answered, "Well, why not? But let's figure out a plan to do this."

As a result of their plans, Audrey flew to the United Nations Youth Environment Forum in New York City, sponsored by Amoco Oil, and circulated a petition asking for a national fund for kids to plant trees. After collecting fifteen hundred signatures from kids all over the United States, she flew to Washington, D.C., and lobbied the U.S. Senate for the student fund. As a result, Congress amended, or changed, the America the Beautiful Act so that youth—and not just adults—could also apply for money for neighborhood improvements in every state.

Audrey received several awards for her work, including the Young Giraffe Award, a national award for students who "stick out their necks." She and some of her classmates flew to Washington, D.C., where they received the President's Environmental Youth Award and got to see President George Bush in person.

She was highlighted, as one of ten students, on a national television program, "Take Me to Your Leaders." Inside, Audrey knew it was all because she had learned to rely on Father in Heaven when she was really young. "I know I couldn't have done any of this without you," she prayed. "Thank you."

In fact, she was so busily engrossed in her tree campaign that she failed to notice any signs of strife at home at all, although they must have been there, falling as the decaying autumn leaves from the honey locust she had planted in her front yard.

She didn't see the problem until it landed right in front of her on Valentine's Day. When she returned home from school, she found a large valentine from her dad to her mother. She read it: "I love you all. I'm sorry." Her mom grabbed a note off the side of the valentine before Audrey could read it. Audrey's stomach churned, and a chill snaked up her back as she wondered what "I'm sorry" could mean.

Her mother sounded breathless as she said, "Audrey, watch the kids for a while. I have to leave for half an hour." She gave no explanation, just grabbed her coat and slipped out the door. Audrey knew that if her mother didn't get back in time for dinner, she could make her homemade cheese sauce for macaroni, but what frightened her was an unnamed fear.

As soon as her mother left, she sneaked into her parents' bedroom and found the note on the bed. The note read, "Dear Ronna, I've noticed some signs. I know you're not happy anymore, and I'm ready to leave if you want me to . . ."

Audrey caught her breath and then burst into choking tears. She kneeled down and prayed. "Please don't let this happen to my family. Help me understand why this is happening. If only I had paid attention . . . maybe I could have done something to stop it."

Then she buried her face in her dog's back and sobbed. Sharmane whimpered and licked her hands. Her dog was old now, blind in both eyes, and suffering from weakened kidneys, but she recognized Audrey. When Audrey arose and walked away, Sharmane scooted across the floor after her, her hind end down.

When her mother returned an hour later, Audrey had gained some control of her emotions. She was ashamed to tell her mother that she had sneaked into her bedroom to read the letter. Audrey also said nothing to her sisters and brothers. When her dad didn't come home that night, her mother made excuses, but Audrey knew. She should have been suspicious when her mother gave her the Judy Blume book *It's Not the End of the World,* which was a story about a girl whose parents get a divorce.

Audrey cried into the checkered quilt long after the lights in her house went off. In the morning, as soon as she heard her father's Datsun truck rattle into the driveway, she raced out the door and threw her arms around him. She inhaled his familiar scent of aftershave as his moustache brushed against her cheek, and he stroked her hair.

Her dad and mom sat all the children down in the living room. "We're having a family meeting," her father explained.

Audrey struggled to swallow tears that choked in her throat. She had been just thinking of herself, but now she had to be strong.

Her dad said, "I have to go away for a while and see if your mother and I can work things out."

Her mother added, "Your daddy and I aren't going to live together anymore."

Audrey's little sister, Darlene, threw herself on the couch and cried, "I know it's our fault because we don't always keep the house clean."

Beverly sobbed, saying, "We promise we won't fight with each other anymore."

"No. No. It's not your fault," her mother reassured them.

Her father also consoled them, "Not at all. You're not to blame."

Audrey felt a nudge from the Holy Ghost, and a strange warmth flowed inside her that told her she must help her family. She pulled Beverly and Darlene close and hugged them. "It will be okay. It's nothing you did or could ever do." Audrey kissed her sisters and brothers, and they looked up at her calm face and started to dry their eyes.

On the following Monday, Audrey's dad came by and picked up Sharmane to take her to the vet because she was dying. Audrey guessed her dad was trying to protect her when she saw the sorrow in her dad's eyes. She suspected her dog would be put to sleep, but she didn't have the strength to focus on it. She felt helpless as a pawn on her dad's chessboard. Some things it seemed you couldn't make happen just by praying.

Audrey stood for a long time at the door. She watched her father's truck back out of the driveway, saw the tires turn, the back end disappear around the corner. She breathed in the odor of car exhaust until it dissipated in the air. She knew she would never see Sharmane again. Was she also losing her father forever?

Here she was just a month later, packing her life in little brown boxes. She didn't understand why her parents were getting a divorce because they were both wonderful people, but she was sure it wasn't her fault. Father in Heaven had given her a feeling of peace that she couldn't describe.

She walked into the kitchen where her mother was shuffling about in house slippers, stuffing dishes into boxes and weeping.

"I'm here, Mom. I'm finished with my packing and can help." Her mother had always shown strength, always stood behind the children. Now Audrey must forget her life at school and help support her mother.

On Friday Audrey rode with her mother and her little brothers and sisters to Menan, Idaho, to live in her grandmother's trailer. There was only one closet to share, and they would have no hot water until the water heater was fixed. They threw out mattresses onto the floor, and her mother fell in an exhausted heap on one of them—worn out from the stress and the long drive. Audrey leaned down and kissed her cheek. In the morning Audrey planned to get up early, organize the younger children, and give them chores to clean up the place. She herself would vacuum and then separate the laundry.

It had been only five weeks since she had seen the valentine, and her entire kaleidoscopic life had been switched to a new pattern. She had left her father behind in Salt Lake City, her grandparents, her friends, her school, her teacher. She hoped her new school wouldn't be too boring, and she swallowed, blinked away tears, and hoped there would still be some adventures ahead for her.

"Help me, Father in Heaven," she prayed. She stepped out of the trailer, looked up at the heavens, and caught her breath. The sky was choked with billions of stars, more stars than she had ever seen before, as if someone had spilled a bag of diamonds across the sky.

She gazed over the acres of flat, grassy fields, the pasture with horses softly neighing, the black ribbon road.

Then an idea hit her—ping—as they always did. "There aren't many trees here." She said it aloud, twirling with outstretched arms. "There are almost no trees," and she hugged herself and smiled. "I'll find a way to get more trees planted in Idaho."

POSTSCRIPT: Audrey organized a "Leaf It to Us" group in Menan and then contacted Idaho senator Larry E. Craig's office for financial help in planting trees in that state. She also joined forces with her old mentor and friend, Dick Klason, the State Forester, who had helped her in Utah, and her former schoolteacher. Together, they joined a national program to encourage young people to plant trees all over the United States.

NOTE: The teacher in this chapter is Barbara Lewis, the author of this book.

Silvanus Sebastian Pillay in Salt Lake City

STRUGGLE FOR JUSTICE

PARENTS
Lawrence Seetha Pillay (deceased) and Florence Pillay

LOCATION OF STORY
Republic of South Africa

When Sebastian's father did not return home in New-castle, Natal, South Africa, his uncles who lived next door began to look for him. They dragged a wooden row-boat into the Ncando River, which ran by their home, searching for his body. Sebastian was only eight years old at that time, but he was old enough to understand that his father had never disappeared before, and he stood in the shadow of bamboo trees outside his tin house and watched.

Neighbors searched across the open fields and among the willows and poplars that grew near the hills. Police-men hunted for one week in bus stations, down dark allies by the iron and steel mills, and around abandoned mine shafts.

Sebastian watched his Granny and mother clinging to each other as they cried in front of the one-room tin house his father had built.

Then he remembered his father's dream that he had shared only a month before. "I see a black coffin," his father had said, "and the coffin is filled with beer and liquor bottles." Sebastian had listened and stored it in his head. Although his father often drank at a bar, had he been trying to tell them that it was wrong to drink these things?

Now he listened to his uncles' shouts as they rowed up the river. His oldest brother Christopher was almost fourteen, and he was allowed to search the river with the men. Sebastian watched their muscled shoulders, glazed with sweat, strain against the oars. They found nothing.

Suddenly his whole East Indian family surrounded Sebastian, between his own tin house and his uncles' brick house. His eyes passed over their faces—his mother, uncles, cousins, aunts, his older brothers, Christopher and Collin, and his three sisters. Everyone threw questions at him.

"Where is the hook, Sebastian?" His granny hung her warm arm around his shoulder.

"I saw you playing with it only a few days ago," Uncle Eugene added. "Can you remember?"

"It is important. We need the hook . . . to drag the river . . . to look for your father." His granny wiped her face with the bottom of her apron, and Sebastian saw fear in her eyes.

"I don't know where it is." Sebastian looked at his toes. He was small for his age, and he felt even smaller now. He wondered if it was his fault they couldn't find his father. Although the sun burned the top of his head with fire, inside he shivered, as if the family's large bellows had blown the heat from him.

He knew it must be his fault, because he could remember swinging the huge hook on a rope high into the willow tree and climbing to the top of its branches, but it wasn't there now. How could he have lost it?

He ran around in circles, past the huge garden plumping up with tomatoes, corn, chilies, pumpkins, and squash. He had been pulling weeds yesterday, but the hook wasn't there.

"Wait! I have found the hook!" Uncle James shouted. "It is by the chicken coop."

Sebastian sighed with relief from his guilt, and he continued his vigil behind the bamboo trees as his uncles and Christopher resumed their search of the river with the hook.

What would his grandfather think of this if he were alive? He remembered the stories of how the old man had been captured by the British in India and brought as a slave to South Africa to work in the sugarcane fields. His grandfather had traveled upon the same ship as Gandhi. His grandfather's people were lost to them because he had only been given a serial number, and his family could not trace his name. And now his father was lost, and they could not trace him either.

When his uncles did find his father in the river only a hundred feet from their home, his brother Christopher stumbled around like a zombie after he witnessed it. His father's body had been tied around the neck with his own tie and anchored to a huge rock to sink him to the bottom of the river. Sebastian learned the details of his father's death by listening to his uncles' angry voices.

"He was in the bar at the Royale Hotel," Uncle Eugene said.

Another uncle added, "Some strangers pretended friendship and left the bar with my brother. Two of the strangers offered to take him home."

"When they reached the river, they hit him over the head with a bottle and killed him for the five rand in his pocket. This we learned, because the strangers brag about their achievement." Uncle Eugene's voice was bitter.

Sebastian saw his father for the last time in a coffin at his uncles' brick house during the funeral, but his father's body was covered up to his neck. Since his father was well-known, hundreds of people came. He had often repaired the neighbors' roofs, helped them lay bricks, and had given away his only car when his best friend got married. He seldom charged anyone for his mechanical skills.

Sebastian stared down at his father's empty face. It didn't look like him. All he could remember was sitting on the side of the Ncando River, fishing together. His dad had rubbed his head and laughed when Sebastian had caught the biggest fish. The pride in his father's eyes had blown up Sebastian's chest. Then his father had hugged him.

Where had his father gone now? Only his body was here. He wished he knew the answers, but he didn't know where to go to find them. Sebastian touched his father's nose lightly, which felt hard and cold. His face was badly damaged, and he didn't look right without his smile. Sebastian pulled up the sides of his father's mouth.

"Sebastian!" his granny's voice slashed at him. "You must not do that." But she stroked his head. Then his mother pulled him close and hugged him.

Everyone looked sad, even Uncle Eugene who was usually so courageous. His uncle's skinny shoulders rounded forward as if they were too heavy for his narrow hips. "Remember that only a week before he died, the river rose from the wrong direction," his uncle said. "It was a sign."

"Yes, the huge red carp swam in from the big sea," Granny added. "Some of the biggest I have ever seen. Strange events like that are signs."

Although the police were able to piece the story together, the murderers were never punished. The murderers bragged that they had bribed a policeman to destroy the evidence.

Sebastian watched his uncles kick the dirt and punch the air with their fists. He watched his mother walk numbly, her face a stiff mask, as she carried water into the tin house. He watched Christopher wandering in circles and silently throwing rocks into the river. Then his brother dropped out of school and left home for Johannesburg, and he was only fourteen years old.

Sebastian gritted his teeth and tossed rocks into the river too. He also threw his fishing stick on the ground.

A week after the funeral, a huge apricot tree fell over and smashed the tin house. Sebastian stared at the pile of collapsed tin and wondered if that were a sign too. He thought about his father's dream, about the red fish, and about the apricot tree and wondered if they were messages from God. But what kind of a God would allow murderers to walk freely in the streets, laughing and boasting, while he stood by the river with no father?

His uncles allowed his family to live in the brick house with them, his aunts, cousins, and Granny. In this house they had two bedrooms in which to live, which seemed large compared to the one-room tin house. Although his mother labored as a machinist making clothing, his family needed the help of welfare to survive.

"Now if everyone would just follow the Ten Commandments," his granny said as the whole family stood together outside the brick house, "we would not fight and argue. We wouldn't have these problems. We would all live in peace."

Granny preached the Bible to him and his sisters more often after the funeral. He often sat at her feet, listening, as she danced her hands and arms about his face like a mesmerizing cobra, describing how Jonah had been swallowed into the belly of a huge whale. She was caught up in the flames of Christian religions that burned across the land and mixed with Hindu and Moslem faiths. She kept Sebastian, his two brothers, and three sisters warned of God's will.

When Sebastian was ten years old, his mother gathered enough money to move to a new housing development in Newcastle. Their tan, cinder-block house was mixed in among fifty other pastel pink, yellow, blue, and lavender square houses across the treeless dirt, and the children called them "Smartie" houses, because the homes reminded them of the familiar candy. They still had no appliances, no clothes washer, no refrigerator, and only a camp stove to cook upon.

Sebastian carried many questions in his head, questions about his father and about justice. He snarled when he first tried to enter a restaurant and found a sign on the door: "No Dogs. No Indians."

Everywhere he looked, he seemed to see injustice. Another time when he rode a bus, a teenager threw a rock right at his head, and no one seemed to notice or care.

When he and his brother Collin, who was one year older, went shopping in Newcastle for a present for their mother, a white clerk stopped them. "What are you doing here? Do you have long fingers?"

"We were not going to steal from you. We came to buy." Sebastian spoke through clenched teeth.

The clerk waved his arms at them. "Get out, you coolies!"

Collin pulled him away, and they left the store. "Leave it alone. We'll go somewhere else."

"It's not fair!" Outside the store Sebastian pulled away from his brother. "At school it is worse. Our Indian school has only a few supplies."

"I know," Collin added, "while white schools have swimming pools, buses—"

"And a big variety of classes. They have languages, modeling, and even topography."

"But the black schools are worse off than us," Collin said. "They even have to buy their own books. The mixed races, the coloreds, aren't any better off than us, either."

"That doesn't make me feel any better." Sebastian stamped in the dirt.

"I'm joining the Indian gang," Collin told Sebastian one afternoon. "It's the only way to get protection and justice. Join with me."

Sebastian paused, wondering if it were the right thing to do, but he admired and loved his brother. "Yes, Christopher, I guess it's the only way to help other kids who get in trouble."

"And to protect each other from beatings." Christopher slapped his shoulder.

Sebastian joined the gang too, but he looked at the tears in his mother's eyes as she begged him against it, and he did not drop out of school. However, the headmaster whacked him many times over his bottom because Sebastian often skipped school. Sebastian began drinking beer and smoking, and he even participated in a few street fights, but inside something told him this wasn't right.

At age fourteen, Sebastian was racing in the shallow part of the river with Collin, and his foot stepped on a broken bottle, practically severing his smallest toe. Four days later, his toe was swollen and rotting. His mother washed it with antiseptic, but it didn't help. "You must go to the doctor," his mother advised.

"But I can't walk on my foot."

"I will carry you." His mother was only five feet tall, the same height as Sebastian, but she hoisted him onto her back and walked, puffing and sweating, many miles

away to a doctor's office and then to the hospital in
Newcastle.

As Sebastian clung to his mother's tiny back and
rested his head upon her swirl of black braids, he guessed
he would never grow six feet tall as his father had been,
but he knew it was the strength of his mother that carried
him, that forced him to stay in school, that taught him to
be honest. He wanted to make her smile again.

He stayed in the hospital for two weeks, and his
mother walked the distance each evening to bring him
favorite dishes—chicken curry with vegetables and rice,
or curry with potatoes and fish, and a drink of Fanta.

As he lay there on hospital sheets, he thought of his
father again, upon the strangeness of the large red carp
and of the apricot tree that had smashed the tin house. He
remembered his father's dream of the coffin filled with
bottles of drink and the message his father must have
been giving them. Then he thought of his tiny mother—
quiet, uncomplaining, strong.

That day in the hospital bed, he changed directions
and vowed to never drink or smoke again. He would bring
a smile to his mother's face. He told his friends of his decision, and six of the eleven gang members, including
Collin, joined him and also changed their habits.

At the same time, he grew skilled at playing soccer
and joined a community competition team. He began running on the high school track team, winning first place
in many heats, and he captured a bronze medal in karate.

When Sebastian was sixteen years old, the Mormon
missionaries stopped next door. His sisters, Lorraine and
Valerie, invited them over to visit with them and his
mother. But as Elder Brent Lee entered the front door
with his companion, Sebastian ducked out the back door
and fled.

"Stay and listen," Valerie encouraged him one day.

"I am not interested in a religion." Sebastian tried to sneak out, but this time Elder Lee met him at the back door and trapped him.

After the discussion, he told Valerie, "That was a pretty good lesson. I liked it when they talked about where we came from and where we are going." He thought about his father. "If this is true, it means our father could still get baptized. It makes sense."

His mother nodded.

Some of his anger evaporated as he listened to the missionaries and as he prayed. God would handle injustice. Sebastian could forget about bribery, about death, about murderers walking free. Slowly he began to feel as if someone had lifted the rock of his father from his own neck.

His mother and three sisters were baptized after about three weeks. A month later, in March, when Sebastian was sixteen years old, he also asked to be baptized. Collin followed his example a few weeks later.

The missionaries continued to visit each day. They spoke of peace, of love and compassion, but they also played, tossed balls, and even chased around the yard. There were forty church members in the Newcastle Branch, including only one other Indian family. They met in a little white house in Newcastle on Sundays. There were only two other young boys in the branch, two and four years younger than he was.

Several families moved away, until there were only six members left. His sisters moved to Johannesburg to live with Christopher. Then the missionaries were pulled out of Newcastle because the branch seemed to be disappearing, but just before the missionaries left, Sebastian was ordained a priest at age seventeen.

One day the branch president walked up to Sebastian and handed him some papers. "Here, if you fill these out, you can go on a mission." Irish O'Moore, Sebastian's employer at the ABD Mining Company and also a Mormon, walked up to him and said, "Look, son, I'll pay for your mission."

"Thanks, Mr. O'Moore, that's very nice of you, but . . . I . . . I . . ." He didn't understand you could refuse to go, and the more he thought about it, the happier he grew about serving a mission. It seemed like the right thing. He was called to serve in the Utah Salt Lake City Mission.

Everything finally seemed to fit into place. Before he left he told his mother, "I know my father's death changed all of our lives. But if he had lived, I don't know if we would have joined the Church. I trust the Lord, and I will go and do the things which the Lord has commanded, for I know he will prepare a way." (See 1 Nephi 3:7.)

Susen Ellen Oehler of East Germany

SUSEN ELLEN OEHLER

THE WALL

PARENT
Hannelore Oehler

LOCATION OF STORY
former East Germany

When Susen was seven years old, her mother warned her: "If your teacher asks you to draw the picture of the clock at school, you must always draw it like this." She pulled a white pad from a chest drawer and placed it on the table in the living room. She drew a round clock with *dots* in place of the numbers.

"Why, Mutti?"

In their small apartment in Cottbus, East Germany, she lowered her voice. "Because you must not let your teacher know that we are watching West German TV for the news. The East German TV stations begin their news reports with this clock with dots, and they only report the greatness of the Communist countries.

"The clock on West German news is a little different." She drew another circle on the paper. "There are *slashes* in place of the numbers, like this." She drew short lines inside the circle clock. "West German news tells us what is happening in the world, but your teacher must not know that we watch it." She held both of Susen's hands and gazed into her face. "Do you understand, Susi?"

Susen nodded her head. It was one of the many rules she must follow.

Her mother added, "We live only eighty miles from Berlin, so they cannot block out the West German stations." Her mother pushed stray blond hairs into her sausage bun.

Then her mother reminded her of poor cousin Michael, who had told a damaging political joke in a pub. Someone passed the information along, and Cousin Michael had gone to prison for two years, right there in the center of Cottbus, and Susen and her mother could not endanger themselves by visiting him.

Susen shivered each time she rode the bus past the high cement prison walls with barbed wire on the top. She could hear the snarling growls of dogs and see their lean bodies patrolling. She didn't like to pass that part of town. Some of the nearby buildings still sagged with jagged, bombed-out holes from the war, like forgotten tramps on the scarred blocks.

"A memory of World War II," her mother whispered. "It would not be good to repair them all, I think. Then we might forget."

Susen knew that this was another forbidden conversation she must not repeat, even though political conflicts appeared remote to her, like distant drums. She learned to keep her lips tight, and when her teacher asked her to draw the clock to show which news report they watched, Susen always drew one with dots for numbers, even though she knew it was a lie.

Susen had always felt uneasy about her room, as though some monster were hiding in the shadows. From the sixth floor of her gray cement apartment, the automobile lights passing across the room at night reminded her of searchlights hunting for an escaped prisoner. This wouldn't have made her shiver so if her mother had been nestled next to her, but her mother's side of the bed was empty and cold every night until long after Susen had finally fallen to sleep.

From the age of three, Susen had known this was the way life had to be. Although she had been born in the The Church of Jesus Christ of Latter-day Saints and had accepted it, one of four thousand five hundred members in East Germany, she had not yet gained a strong testimony, nor had she needed to make difficult choices.

For now she knew there were rules she had to follow that could not be bent, such as her mother having to work each day at the architect's office until four P.M. and then attending trade school in the evening in order to become an industrial engineer. So every evening her mother left for school, and Susen had to put herself to bed alone at seven.

When Susen turned five years old, she was tall and clever and discovered she could unlock the front door of her two-room apartment, knock on Mrs. Noack's door, and whine, "My mama is not home, and I'm scared."

Mrs. Noack cradled her. "Don't be afraid, little one. Come, let's go tuck you back into bed, and if you're a big girl and stop crying, I might be able to find some nice sweet chocolate in my pocket." Mrs. Noack marched ahead, her flowered dress swaying above sturdy, black shoes.

The chocolate bribe always hooked her. She knew that Mrs. Noack had relatives in Western Germany and was somehow able to get creamy, mouth-watering chocolate that was very different from the nasty, waxy stuff her mother could buy at the Delikat. Even at five, she learned that if you had clothes and goods from the West, others thought you were very special.

Susen continued to visit Mrs. Noack all through her school career, stopping in to chatter about school or Primary. Sometimes Mrs. Noack attended Relief Society work meetings with Susen's mom.

One day Susen rushed in breathless and said, "The Russian army children visited our school again today."

Mrs. Noack raised her eyebrows.

"Today we played games with them and sang Communist songs." Susen propped her chin in cupped hands, seated at Mrs. Noack's small table in the living room.

Mrs. Noack poured steaming hot chocolate into a stoneware cup. "What games did you play with these Russian children?"

"Where you put chairs in the middle of the room and then keep taking one until no one has a place to sit."

"Sounds like a political game." Mrs. Noack smiled as she sat down beside her.

"What? I don't understand."

Mrs. Noack did not answer, but she pursed her lips. The carved grandfather's clock against the cement wall chimed three times. A thin echo hung in the air, then slipped away.

Susen and her mother continued to watch West German news and learned of various escape attempts over the Berlin Wall. One brave family drifted over in a hot-air balloon. Another rammed through the Wall in a steel-plated car; some climbed over. Bullets riddled many of their bodies as they attempted to escape, and flowered wreaths lined the Wall in memory of those who failed.

Susen was curious about the Western world, but since they had no close relatives living there, it seemed far away from her. Besides, she loved her school and her apartment on the Stadtpromenade. From her cheerful red balcony, she looked out over the city at the large A-framed electrical scaffolds, standing like metal giants with legs straddled. Coal-processing plants belched out smoke and painted a thin layer of gray soot over buildings, houses, streets, and trees.

When the muted sun shone through this hazy veil, her industrial city seemed to Susen like a dusty Renaissance painting. She could see no conflict with her country while eating chocolate with Mrs. Noack. She didn't understand why people hurled themselves against the Wall like mad dogs trying to escape a kennel.

Each afternoon as her mother returned from the architect's office at four, Susen clung to her hand and scampered downstairs to shop for sausages and bread at the Delikat. Sometimes they entered the Jugendmode to buy her something new to wear to school.

"I want pants like Christiane," she always begged. Her mother smiled and usually bought the pants and then allowed her to wear her long, blond hair straight down her back. Susen had no patience for curls.

She asked her mother, "Why don't we buy an automobile?" She pointed at a small cluster of cars parked outside the shopping area.

"An automobile? What next? You will probably ask for a phone."

"But why not, Mutti?"

"Because, little one, we do not have enough money. Besides, you must wait ten years for a phone, fifteen years or more to get a car." She smiled and squeezed Susen's hand. "You will be all grown up by then, I think."

Susen accepted it as another rule. You go to school. You go to church. You draw dots for the numbers when your teacher asks you which clock, and you can't have an automobile.

She really didn't care that they didn't have an automobile. Christiane didn't have one either or any of her other friends. Her worst problem was when other school children called her "Fette Susen" because she was chubby, everyone except Christiane who lived on the seventh floor of the same apartment.

Susen thought Christiane looked like a boy with her short hair and boy pants, and she had a loud voice. When Christiane walked, she threw out her arms in parenthesis at her sides, like a wrestler, and Christiane could kick the soccer ball farther than most of the boys at school.

"Will you come to Primary with me?" Susen invited Christiane one day after school.

"Yes, but your church is strange. It doesn't look like a church."

Susen felt defensive. She thought that the Mormon Cottbus Ward was beautiful. "I think it's pretty," she disagreed.

Christiane giggled. "But it's just an old restaurant. My mother told me it used to be called 'To the Gray Monkey.'"

So when Susen attended Bible lessons with Christiane, she was envious as they climbed the steps into a huge gothic church, its spires and arches pointing up like praying hands. But inside, when her friend recited rote answers to questions, Susen didn't feel anything. She didn't feel the warmth that filled her chest when her mother stood and bore her testimony in the Cottbus Ward or when Brother Lehnig spoke about listening to the still, small voice.

Later, while eating bratwurst and sauerkraut at dinner with her mother, she said, "It's not from the heart. It is memorized, like saying a poem."

"I know that. It doesn't matter how fancy a church is,

it is what happens inside the heart that invites the Spirit there."

Susen smiled. She licked her finger and ran it around the rim of the crystal glass to make it sing. Sometimes if she got just the right pitch, she could make the other crystal glasses—which covered every table and mantle in the living room—ring out in a thin chorus.

"Susen, you're not listening." Her mother touched the rim of the glass, and the music stopped. "When you are old enough to attend youth conferences you will meet in other places similar to the Cottbus Ward, like the old cinema in Leipzig and the old factory in Karl Marx Stadt.

"And something else you should be grateful for." Her mother scooped beans, carrots, and potatoes onto Susen's plate. "Your grandparent's garden. The grocery stores—they have little fresh produce, and when it *is* there, it is bruised and spoiling."

Susen sank her teeth into the buttered potatoes. She loved to eat the food and didn't mind weeding the acre of land that was her grandparents' garden, where she could also play soccer with her cousins. None of them called her "Fette Susen."

One day after weeding for two hours, she traipsed into her grandparents small stucco house and looked in the tall mirror at the roundness of her body. "Why must I be fat?" she moaned.

"Don't worry, sweet one," her grandfather said as he hugged her. One of his legs was shorter than the other, and he always limped. "When you grow taller and your baby fat stretches out over your body, you will become slim and beautiful like me." He laughed and tapped his short leg.

She did start to grow slim as she turned eleven. She noticed it one day when she tied the red scarf around her neck and tucked her white shirt into the blue pants, her

uniform as a member of the Communist youth organization, the *Thaelmann Pioniere Gruppe.*

She told herself she was lighter as she skipped across
the street to school with Christiane. Then she stopped
short, yanked Christiane by the arm, and stood behind
the chestnut tree as Russian soldiers marched past. She
never felt comfortable around them when they paraded up
and down the Stadtpromenade in their loden green uni-
forms, pistols at their waists or rifles at their sides. Since
a branch of the Russian army was housed in a brick building on the same street, they passed her apartment often.
Mostly she ignored them as she would gray clouds moving
overhead. She never spoke to them.

However, today from the safety of the chestnut tree,
she and Christiane waited as fifty soldiers marched by.
The unison smack of one hundred, leather, knee-high
boots reminded her of the whack of the headmaster's
ruler. For the first time she looked into their eyes, and
she saw no laughter, and the breath caught in her throat.

It wasn't until Susen turned sixteen that she first recognized how tightly her freedom was controlled. She had
finished middle school and wanted to transfer to a specialized school to study to be a teacher. She wrote on the
application that she wished to teach German and English
to teenaged students.

When Susen took her application to her high school
teacher to be approved, her teacher shook her head sadly.
"I can't sign this."

"But why not?" Susen asked.

"Because, Susen, I know that you are a Mormon. Is
that correct?" She sat at a desk in the teacher's room.

Susen felt panic rising in her throat.

"You see, Susen, in order to be a teacher you have to
teach atheism, or disbelief in God. Atheism is the state

religion. To become a teacher, you will have to deny your religion and your belief in God. Are you prepared to do this?"

Susen ran home and buried her face in the *Feder-decke*—the feathered quilt—on her bed and cried until her mother returned from work. "I don't understand this, Mutti. Why was I born here? Why couldn't I live some-where else—some place where I don't have a problem with my religion?"

Her mother rubbed Susen's back. "This is a wonderful country, and many valiant people live here, both in and out of the government, and you have a purpose in being here. Somehow things will work out, Susi."

"No. That isn't good enough. I want to be a teacher." She banged her fist on the bed. "Why can't I just be what I want to be? That isn't asking for too much, is it?"

"Pray about it, Susen. That is all I can say."

Susen asked herself, "Do I care that much about my religion to give up my chance to teach?" She prayed. She prayed into the evening, and still she wasn't sure.

She prayed for two days before she received an answer, which came in the form of a comforting peace. Her place was in East Germany. She had always known it, never yearning for the Western world like many of her friends, who would gladly have given up a year of their lives for one pair of Western jeans.

She hugged her mother and explained, "Mutti, I know that the Church is more important to me than anything, and I know that whatever happens will be the way it is supposed to be. I have gained a lot of trust in Heavenly Father now, and I believe this is the beginning of a stronger testimony."

So Susen wrote on her application that she wanted to go into economics instead of teaching, though it was not what she wanted to write. She sensed that she had just

swept her problem under the rug and would see it again
some day.

Susen graduated from the high school and prepared to
ride the train to Magdeburg, five hours away, where she
would attend a specialized school to study economics. She
hugged her mother, Christiane, Mrs. Noack, and her
grandparents and set off alone on the train.

While she was away at school, her grandmother died
of heart problems, and her beautiful grandfather died
soon after, of a broken heart. Mrs. Noack would also die of
cancer before long. Susen yearned for the old days when
her greatest worry was how to go to sleep alone and when
a cup of hot chocolate satisfied her. She knew she had just
crossed a ravine. Always before she had been able to run
back to her mom, Mrs. Noack, or her grandparents, but
she could not jump backward anymore. She must stand
on her own feet.

During the time that Susen studied economics, she
saw certain conditions in East Germany grow worse. The
meager supply of produce disappeared from the shelves.
Clothing vanished from racks. She stood in lines for hours
at a time to get bread or meat.

On TV she learned of Gorbachev's theory of pere-
stroika, the economic and government reform that
included loosening restrictions with the Western world.
She no longer had to pretend she watched only Eastern
news, as the Communist government had given up trying
to restrict the news.

She and her classmates discussed the pros and cons of
socialism and communism openly with their philosophy
teacher. "Why is it so difficult to get a visa to a Western
country if you are young?" a student asked.

Another student said, "I think it is because if you are
sixty or sixty-five, the government would like you to leave

so that you are not a burden in your old age, but if you are young, the government wants you to stay here and contribute."

"Or maybe they don't want us to know how good things are in the West." Susen spoke before she realized what she had said. Then she covered her mouth and shivered, because she had always kept tight lips, and now she feared what might happen.

When she returned home for the summer, her mother explained with a worried face, "A policeman has called me at work and asked many questions about you."

Susen felt a chill, and she sensed that the distant drumming fear she had once felt was closer.

A couple of days later she was in her apartment alone when someone knocked at her door. Susen hesitated a moment, then opened the door.

A tall man stood in the doorway. "I am from the police," he said, showing her his photo identification card.

Susen's face drained pale.

"Happy birthday, Susen," he said, and he walked into the apartment without an invitation.

Susen's heart beat rapidly. How had he known she had just had her twentieth birthday?

The man fired questions at her and then answered them before she could speak. He seemed to know everything about her and her mother. He knew her friends, talked about her classes, her daily schedule. He even asked her about the Mormon Church, and Susen rummaged in her chest drawer and found a card that listed the Articles of Faith and gave it to him.

After much questioning, Susen realized that he wanted information about a man she knew who sold computers in Switzerland and that he probably wasn't really interested in her at all. She saw fifty German marks in his bag and realized with a jolt that he had been prepared to bribe her for information. She wondered what her acquaintance in Switzerland might have done, or if this policeman simply wanted to buy a computer from him.

When she could tell him nothing, the man left and never called again, but now that she knew how much information the police collected on people, she tightened her lips again and began a habit of looking behind her back when she walked.

As the economy continued to slump, Susen heard women complain in the Delikat that their children needed milk to grow, while gray, bent people grumbled that they couldn't get enough food to stay alive. No one had enough money. The citizens moaned and grumbled, demanding that the government do something.

In the midst of the confusion, Susen applied for a visa to travel to the city of Kiel in West Germany to attend a wedding anniversary of her friends, Heinz and Sigrid. She was astonished when she actually received the visa. She knew that permission to travel to the West for special family events had been unheard of prior to the past few years of the Socialist era.

She whispered quietly with her mother the night before she was to board the train on her first trip out of East Germany.

"You know, Susi. You don't have to come back." Her mother clasped Susen's hands in hers.

Susen protested, "What? But I can't leave you."

"I am getting older, and it doesn't matter. You are young, and I will understand if you decide to defect and stay there. You would probably have a better life."

"But . . ."

Her mother covered Susen's lips with her fingertips. "Hush, child. Don't speak now. Only think about it."

Susen's stomach twisted, for it was true that she might never again receive such an opportunity.

When she stepped off the train in Kiel, West Germany, Susen wondered if she were dreaming. Color was splashed everywhere. Pastel-colored flowers spilled over hundreds of flower boxes on chalet balconies. Thousands of cars—some even tomato red—honked and zoomed everywhere.

The stores sold facial creams, hair coloring, perfumes, jeans, and leather jackets that she had never seen before. Outside of delicatessens, baskets of fruits and vegetables bulged with fresh carrots, broccoli, leeks, chicory, bananas, apples, cherries, and grapes.

She shopped for shoes, attended cinemas, danced, and laughed with Heinz and Sigrid. She knew she could stay there and be happy, but should she go home? She prayed each day for an answer, and even as she prayed, she knew what she must do.

"Why don't you stay here?" Sigrid begged.

Heinz added, "You know you would have a better future here with more choices, and you might never be able to come back. This may be your one chance."

After four weeks of deliberation, she boarded the return train, her luggage heavier with Western goods and her thoughts heavier with memories, but her heart beating evenly. She told herself, "I am crazy to be going back, but I love the people, and I know my place is in East Germany." As the train chugged over the border, something told her it was not the last time she would see West Germany.

Back in Cottbus, she watched the whirlwind of political events every evening on the Western news. By August 1989, Poland elected its first noncommunist government since World War II. In October, the Hungarians disbanded the Communist party and planned for free elections. The same month, East Germany's Communist hardliner, President Erick Honecker, resigned.

Susen listened as neighbors asked, "What does this mean?"

"Who cares? We still have no food." They shook their heads.

East Germans taking refuge in West German embassies in Poland and Czechoslovakia begged for visas into West Germany. Requests for visas and demands for change piled up in stacks on government desks.

Gorbachev had earlier weakened the position of East Germany's Communist party by stating he wouldn't intervene in the internal affairs of the country and was planning withdrawal of Russian troops.

On November 9, 1989, Susen sat watching the news in Sister Kossok's living room after a Church institute class. Guenter Schabowski, press speaker and member of the Politburo, announced the bombshell news: the East German borders were now open for travel to the West.

"What? Can this be true? Does it mean there will be no more Berlin Wall?" The Wall had always been there, more constant it seemed than the change of seasons. To have it disappear suddenly seemed inconceivable. So she listened for details. It was true. Susen had not heard incorrectly. She turned and hugged Sister Kossok, while they cried with happiness.

Shortly after, Susen learned that the intention of the announcement might not have been to open the borders for everyone. Schabowski had read a comment written by Egon Krenz, the new General Secretary, which only stated his intent to *address* the border problem, but Schabowski had misinterpreted it to mean that the borders were opened.

At first Susen feared Communist leaders would correct the mistake, and her heart sank. However, under the pressure of mass demonstrations and emigration, the Communist party was unable to retract the statement. Within hours of the announcement, thousands of Germans converged upon the Berlin Wall, driving and walking through from both sides. They shouted, cupped each other's faces, and kissed. West Germans with musical instruments strummed and tooted in the streets. They poured champagne, clinked glasses, and handed armfuls of flowers to relatives and to East German border guards.

East Germans crossing to the West gazed about in a daze, as though awakened from a deep sleep, at the progress of their cousins. Soon after, they began chipping and pounding at the Wall with hammers and bashing at it with crowbars as East and West Germans symbolically clasped hands through holes.

Susen exclaimed to her mother, "This is wonderful! This 'mistake' is an answer to prayers. Do you realize what this means, Mutti?"

Her mother nodded. "Freedom," she replied.

"More than that. Think of it. Now the Church can grow."

Susen continued to watch the sequence of events on the Western news. She cheered in December when parliament abolished the Communist monopoly on power and the leadership resigned. She believed that God had inspired it all. She ran around her apartment with wet fingers and set all the crystalware ringing together. The free news and the clock with "slashes" instead of "dots" had resonated over the Wall, setting the Eastern world vibrating with freedom.

After the fall of the Berlin Wall, Susen was called to serve in the Utah Salt Lake City Mission as the first missionary from the Cottbus Ward since her mother had served there in East Germany thirty years before.

Susen wrote in her journal: "When the Communist

party fell apart, I saw people flounder who didn't have any religion to hold onto. They were lost. I knew I had a responsibility to share the blessings of my church with others. And in spite of everything, as a missionary now I am finally a teacher."

Mable and Herald Hammond
beside Richard and his new bike

Herald Hammond, left, and Richard Glatzer, right

RICHARD GLATZER

HOMELESS

PARENTS
Richard and Betty Glatzer

LOCATION OF STORY
Eugene, Oregon; Idaho City, Idaho; and Salt Lake City, Utah

Eight-year-old Richard looked down at the five dollar bill cupped in his hand, the money he had received for mowing a neighbor's lawn in Eugene, Oregon. The freckles stretched on his smiling cheeks because he could buy a tire for his bike now. Then his smile faded. But what about food?

He thought of his famished stomach and imagined the sides pressing together like a deflated balloon, but he was used to hunger. Toward the end of the month, when the food stamps ran out and all that was left was what the Salvation Army could give them, he sometimes ate only one meal a day.

He thought of his little sister, Heather, only five years old, and remembered listening to her hungry cries in bed last night. Since his stomach was older than Heather's, he could will it to be quiet and go to sleep, but thinking of his sister, he clinched the bill into a wad and kicked a rock all the way to the food market.

He scurried past the in-store bakery and smelled the

111

rising bread dough. Wiping his lips, he picked up a loaf of white bread, then snatched a box of macaroni and cheese and juggled a gallon of milk in his arm. At the checkout counter, he counted his money and added one Snickers bar.

He carried his purchases—milk carton in one arm and bread and macaroni slung over his shoulder like a plastic Santa sack—to his home on Eighth Street, across from the park. He hopped up the steps to their three-story brick house, which the Episcopal Church had donated for their use, and where Richard had a bedroom of his own on the third floor. All the furniture, linens, and bedding were thrown together like mismatched socks, and Richard loved it.

As he placed the sack on the kitchen table, Heather and David, his nine-year-old brother, tore into it, but Richard grabbed the Snickers bar and gave it to Heather. He pushed his dark, sweaty hair away from his forehead and beamed. Tonight they would eat.

He understood his dad's health problem. Although his father had attended Cornell University, midway through his college career he had developed diverticulosis, a disease of the digestive track. He had undergone many surgeries, and most of his intestines had been removed. His mother stayed home to take care of his invalid dad; so the family survived on welfare.

His dad was always around to help him with homework, but Richard longed to go fishing with his father or to throw a baseball around. Richard learned how to garden, and he constantly foraged the neighborhood for gardening and mowing jobs to buy food.

Later that night, with stomachs stretched out with bread and macaroni, Richard grabbed David by the sleeve and said, "Come on. It's garbage pickup tomorrow."

"I'm coming," David called, ambling behind him on long, grasshopper legs.

"Maybe we can find a tire for the bike."

Richard and his brother prowled the streets as dusk smeared the outlines of stores—the Dairy Mart, the vacuum and TV repair shops. Metal business marquees sagged over the sidewalks like stooped shoulders. They passed dented silver garbage cans and rooted in junk piles behind apartment houses.

"Let's go to the bicycle shop." Richard's wiry body skipped ahead.

"Yeah, they throw out lots of good stuff."

Richard found the discarded tire he needed—and bike gears as a bonus—behind the bicycle shop. Richard had all the pieces he needed to make his bike. He had found an old bike frame thrown outside an apartment building and a set of handle bars (only slightly bent) in a trash can. Several previous visits to the bicycle shop had yielded unwanted nuts, bolts, chains, and an only slightly ripped seat outside the shop.

Richard held his head high, wind cooling the dampness of his tousled hair, as he careened around corners on his patchwork bike. He let David and his best friend, Rickie Wagner, ride the bike also. Sometimes he saved a few dollars from his lawn jobs, and he and David or Rickie doubled up on the bike to go swimming in Springfield, a few miles away.

When his father's illness grew worse, Richard's parents planned to move to Idaho, where physicians at the Intermountain Hospital in Idaho City would attempt to treat his illness. Richard helped his family pack the U-Haul, but there was no room for his patchwork bike.

He stared at his masterpiece, rubbed the handlebars, and polished the rusty chrome with Vasoline. Then he rode it over to Rickie's house and gave it to him. He refused to cry. He could will his eyes to hold back the tears, but he didn't dare look back as he walked away from Rickie's house.

Richard's family lived two weeks in one room in the homeless shelter in Idaho City and then moved into welfare housing. His father suffered from many hernias, or protrusions of his intestines through his abdominal wall. As a result of his worsening condition, when Richard was fourteen years old, he and his family moved to Salt Lake City, where his father's hernias were operated on at the University of Utah Medical Center.

The Jewish Community Center housed his family in a motel for a few weeks, and then they moved into the Salt Lake City homeless shelter. Once again the family lived in one room, and the children had to return to the room by 8:00 P.M. and remain there. They were not allowed to sit out in the family-room area to watch TV after that hour. The toys consisted mostly of broken cars and trucks for younger children and Dr. Seuss books that didn't interest Richard. He kept track of Heather by playing Monopoly with her in the shelter and made David help straighten the room when their parents were gone, but in spite of Richard's boredom, he knew it was nice of people to help them like that.

Because the shelter had no school for teens, Richard attended a public junior high school, but he was not there long enough to make new friends. A local television station highlighted his family in a story of the homeless shelter, and as a result, some students at the school shot sarcastic comments at Richard.

"Whoa! I saw you on TV."

"You live in the homeless shelter, huh? Cool."

"Yeah, Richard Glatzer, the big movie-star dude of the homeless shelter."

"I do most of my things without people anyway," Richard told himself. "I don't care what they say. I can will myself to do this." However, he walked along the edges of the school halls alone, his face looking downward at the scuffed floor tiles.

While Richard was at the homeless shelter, the Mormon missionaries visited. Richard perked his head up, immediately interested. He liked the clean, pressed-suit look of Elder Hardy from Canada and Elder Boyer from California. Other shelter residents listened at first, but they blew away like butterflies from a windshield. Only Richard hung on.

He remembered the times he had attended different Protestant churches when he lived in Eugene and his attempts to get David or Rickie to attend with him. Now he smiled eagerly at these new missionaries, ate ice cream with them, and sat glued to his chair, listening to their lessons and stories. The missionaries took him for a tour of Temple Square and gave him a copy of the Book of Mormon.

One late afternoon he lay on the bed in his family's shelter room and stared at the ceiling with his Book of Mormon resting open-faced over his stomach. He only understood some of the passages, but the book gave him a good feeling to read it. His family was out in the common area, watching TV.

"Please, God," he spoke aloud, "tell me if this is true. I feel happy when I'm with the missionaries. I know this is not my father's fault, but I don't want to live like this. I want to do better. I think I want to join this church."

Richard felt peace slowly seep through him, and he suddenly wanted to cheer. He had his answer.

When his parents returned to their room, Richard announced, "I'm going to join the Mormon Church. No matter what anyone says, I'm going to."

"Hold on," his mother said. She looked tired, her eyes hammocked in dark circles.

His dad hobbled over to a broken-down chair. He sat slowly, as though it pained him. "You've got to think about what you'd be getting into first, Son. That's a strange religion. Why not the Jewish religion or some other Protestant faith?"

"No!" Richard persisted. "I want to join the Mormon Church. I've even prayed about it."

Because they could see that it might help him, his parents finally relented and allowed him to join, but they didn't attend his baptism in the Tabernacle on Temple Square.

Richard lost track of the missionaries when his family moved to an apartment in south Salt Lake County funded with the help of social security and welfare. He began attending another school as a seventh grader, although he was the same age as many ninth graders. This time as he walked the sides of the halls like a shadow, other students noticed his handsome face, his eager grin, his rosy complexion. Although Richard could handle being alone, his heart raced when they invited him to go with them after school.

Before Richard knew what had happened, these new friends had pulled him into a gang and threatened to beat the tar out of him if he tried to escape. He began skipping school and stopped doing his homework. He tried smoking cigarettes and marijuana, but his throat choked on the smoke, and he threw the drugs into the garbage. His stomach felt empty again when he stared at his new "friends" hanging around in the alleys, and he knew he'd reached the end of another dead-end street.

On a Friday afternoon in the spring, he decided to go somewhere, anywhere, so that he wouldn't have to hang out on the streets. He wished he still had his old bike, but other kids would probably just poke fun at it. Someday, when he had a good job, he was going to buy himself a beautiful bike. He boarded the city bus and rode back to the vicinity of the homeless shelter.

He wandered past a store with a toy-car display, stopped, and pressed his palms against the windows. His eyes landed on a black-and-white remote-control car, but the price tag read $139.95. His hands slid off the window, and he stuffed them in his pockets.

He passed a transient leaning against a warehouse wall. Tufts of hair stuck out from his mostly bald head, and his front teeth reminded Richard of a jagged picket fence. The man held a cup and wore a cardboard sign hanging around his neck that said, "Will werk for food."

Suddenly Richard felt as if he were clawing at the sides of a deep pit and he couldn't get out. His heart raced, and he took a deep breath and ran. "I've got to find a job," Richard thought. "Help me find a job," he prayed.

He jogged down two blocks before a warehouse caught his attention. A huge clown was painted on the side of the building with a sign, "Twirl Town Toys." He remembered it was the same place David had earned a few dollars cleaning the parking lot when they had lived at the shelter.

Richard didn't waste any time but tucked his shirt in his trousers and pushed the glass door open. "Do you have a job I can do," he asked?

An older man sat on a table, talking with a younger man in overalls. He introduced himself as Herald Hammond, owner of Twirl Town Toys. Herald smiled. "Why do you need a job?" He pulled off a baseball cap and scratched the top of his partly bald head.

"My brother, David, did a job for you last winter when I was in the homeless shelter." Richard wiped sweaty hands on his jeans and searched for convincing words.

"And I need a job, because I don't want to be poor anymore. You don't even have to pay me. I'll be willing to work for free, just to have something to do."

"I don't know. Do you think we've got anything for this kid to do?" Herald grinned, his kindly eyes pulling tight from smile wrinkles as he winked at the other man.

"Could sack some kick balls," the employee answered.

"Come on." Herald pulled his arm around Richard's neck and escorted him to the back of the warehouse, where Richard helped to bag a couple thousand balls, twenty-four to a bag, for shipment to various stores.

At the end of the day he asked Herald if he could come back again.

"How about next Monday?" Herald asked. Then he gave Richard two dollars.

Richard began working for Herald every day after school. He cleaned his storage shelves and boxed orders of toy cars, games, and Barbie dolls to be trucked to a variety of drug and department stores. He took his first check and bought himself some new shorts and a shirt, but he also bought Heather some jeans and a dressy blouse with lace around the collar.

He worked for Herald every chance he could get. He never wanted to go back to the gang, and this gave him an excuse. When he received a check for eighty dollars, he gave half of it to his parents to buy food, and he continued to divide his checks with them.

Later in the summer, Richard went camping with Herald's family at Willard Bay, and Herald brought his boat. "It's easy to ski, Richard," Herald encouraged him. "Just watch, and I'll do a demo for you." Herald splashed off the side of the boat and did a clown routine on his skis. He flipped around on one ski, held the rope with his toe, arms folded and looking bored. Then Herald donned a wig and eighteen-inch sunglasses and shot everyone with his long-distance squirt gun. Richard laughed and held his sides until they ached.

It looked pretty easy to Richard. After Herald's example, he got up on the skis on the first try, and as he skimmed across the glasslike water, he felt free as a kite tethered to Herald's boat.

In the evening he sat in the sand and stuffed himself with Mable Hammond's barbecued chicken, potato salad, watermelon, and brownies dripping with chocolate. He licked his fingers and looked up at Mable, who stood there smiling, watching him wolf down the food. He wiped smears of barbecue sauce from his mouth with a paper napkin. "Thanks so much," he said. "I've never had so much fun before."

Herald put his arm around Mable, and Richard saw them watching him. He knew he was just one of ten different young people they had taken into their home to help over the years, along with eight children of their own. He sensed that somehow it might be fun for them, too, to watch his enthusiasm for skiing, working, eating.

When they drove down the Interstate on the way back to Salt Lake, Richard stretched out in the van. Although he wanted to go home to see his family, he also didn't want to go home. If he could stay with Herald and Mable, he could start a new life.

He swallowed hard and blurted out, "Herald, can I come home with you?" He shocked himself with his own outburst.

Herald's eyes widened. "Why do you want to go home with me? I'm a Mormon, and I'm just going to church in the morning."

Richard sat straight up. "Wow! I'm a Mormon too. I joined when I was in the homeless shelter, and I don't have anyone to go to church with."

Herald grinned and looked at Mable, who nodded and

squeezed his hand. So Richard began staying weekends with the Hammonds and working with Herald. It was still difficult, though, for him to avoid gang members and shuttle back and forth.

Finally, Richard asked the Hammonds if he could live with them, and they consented if it was okay with his parents. When Richard called to get permission from his parents, they refused.

"We love you, Richard," his father reminded him.

"You're the one who cleans up and takes care of things. How can we get along without you?" his mother said, sniffing.

Heather cried over the phone, "I miss you, Richard. Come home."

"I love all of you too," he cried. He felt stretched thin in two directions. "But this is the first time in my life I'm having fun," he stammered, his eyes blurring. "I can't explain it, but I can't make it there. I can't do it. The gang members won't leave me alone. Maybe I can help out, but first I have to do it myself."

His parents cried some more but finally consented. They agreed he needed to attend school in another neighborhood away from the gang members, and they worked out an arrangement with the Hammonds for Richard to visit home on weekends. Richard was fifteen when he began living with Herald and Mable on a more full-time basis.

His father said, "I can't help what has happened to my body, but you can design what happens to you, and we want the best opportunities for you."

Richard learned new customs at the Hammonds. Herald expected him to be in the house each evening by 8:30. Richard didn't mind. He struggled with his homework because he hadn't developed consistent study habits.

He attended summer school to make up for some of his credits lost in moving around.

At church he passed the sacrament and began to talk about going on a mission when he was older. He attended youth conference at Camp Williams, a camp for the National Guard and Army Reservists, where he voluntarily cleaned the barracks the 120 youth had occupied.

One day Herald told Richard to follow him to the garage, that he had a surprise for him. Richard scurried behind Herald. "What is it?" He pulled on Herald's arm. "Is it a dog?"

Herald looked back over his shoulder and smiled a sneaky grin.

When Richard stepped into the garage, his mouth fell open. There stood a used but shiny, black mountain sport bike leaning against the wall. His eyes widened, hungry and eager. He remembered his patchwork bike and willed himself not to cry again, but this time he didn't succeed.

Later Richard straddled his new bike and leaned forward on the handle. "Herald," he said, "I've got to tell you something. You and Mable are the best things that have ever happened to me in all my life. I'm glad for the chance to live here and go to school."

He looked over his shoulder, as though hunting for a memory. "I know how it hurts to be hungry. I haven't forgotten that." He grasped the handlebars until his knuckles turned white. "And I still worry about my family. Maybe someday, I can help them."

Then he relaxed his fists and leaned on one leg. "I promise you I'm going to work hard, because I never want to be homeless again."

John Meranda and Ashley Griffin,
the baby whose life John saved

John Meranda shaking hands with President George Bush

JOHN MERANDA

SAVING A BABY

PARENTS

Thomas E. and Mary Lynne Meranda

LOCATION OF STORY

Lebanon, Indiana

W ill you boys stop it!" John's mother stamped into the living room, her mouth stretched into a thin line. "Get control before you break something."

Thirteen-year-old John Meranda grabbed his brother, Troy, by the leg and then tumbled over the carpet, banging into a wooden end table in their Indiana home. He crashed right into his mother's tapping foot, then looked up and grinned sheepishly.

"Have you finished your newspaper collections yet? You can't just deliver the *Lebanon Reporter*. You collect, too. Remember?" She winked at him.

"We're just playing." John hung onto Troy's shirt as Troy tried to drag himself away from John's clutches. John was in no hurry and didn't expect anything exciting to happen this lazy Friday evening.

He saw his mother's stare as she surveyed the books scattered across the carpet. "And, John, would you please put all these books away? You know, I think you're the only kid in Lebanon Middle School who had his school library card revoked for *over*use.

"John, I'm talking to you." She grabbed his toe. "I'm glad you like to read. Goodness knows you read everything but the dictionary."

"Oh, I like that too." John gasped as his twenty-pound tabby cat pounced on his chest, practically knocking the wind out of him, and kneaded her panther-sized paws on his shirt. John giggled and pushed her away.

His mother disappeared into the kitchen and returned with a wooden paddle. "All right, you two. Get going." She whopped John and his brother teasingly on their bottoms. "Move it! And this time, John, don't give all your money away. You don't have to pay everyone else's newspaper bills. You may be a fantastic delivery boy, but you're not much of a collector."

John grumbled and pulled on his Mets cap. "Come on, Troy." Although Troy was four years younger than he, his little brother outweighed him by ten pounds. John always complained that he weighed only seventy pounds in a padded snowsuit and that he stood barely over four feet tall.

He glanced over his shoulder as he leaped down the front porch steps and saw his mother smiling and shaking her head as she watched them leave. "And don't take two hours, either. You don't need to visit with everyone."

However, delivering papers was a social activity for John. He usually read the *Lebanon Reporter* first, spreading it all over his bedroom floor. He sometimes clipped out the political cartoons and a few interesting articles so that he could report the news as he delivered the paper to each of his customers. With over forty clients, that could take an entire day.

He stopped regularly at Leo Endres's house, a ninety-year-old gentleman who sat in his overstuffed chair by

the front door and waited for visitors. Sometimes Leo
allowed John to ride his Toro lawn mower and cut the
grass, and sometimes John took some of his mother's stew
to Leo for dinner. When money was tight for his old friend,
he sometimes paid for Leo's newspapers out of his own
pocket.

John also visited with a middle-aged man who was
recovering from a stroke and bypass heart surgery. The
man raised wild birds, and John liked to feed the quail,
bobwhites, and pheasants and to watch the mallards waddle
like windup toys.

Today John took off with determination to get the job
done quickly because he hated collecting. It was just an
ordinary April evening in central Indiana. The Lebanon
humidity had already cranked up and was saturating the
city with sticky air. The boys jostled down East Main
Street past the street maples and entered a brick apartment building. "Come on, Troy," John called. "Come on in
with me."

John banged his knuckles on apartment number 1.

"This is boring. These guys are never home." Troy
leaned against the dark mahogany wall.

Then John heard a cry, but it didn't come from number 1. He looked at Troy, then across the hall. He heard a
frantic voice, a child's voice repeating, "Please don't be
dead, Ashley. Please don't be dead."

Although John thought it was probably none of his
business, his ears perked up. After all, this was his paper
route. John turned and banged on the door across the
hall. When he heard the lock click, he pushed the door
open, and a little girl stepped aside. Across the room, a
confused-looking babysitter was holding a baby against
her chest. The baby's face was as blue as a plum.

John's mind shot back to the basic first-aid training in

Scouts. What was he supposed to do for choking? A good Scout should always be prepared.

The baby-sitter threw him a helpless look and shrugged in frustration.

"Quick! Turn the baby over," John ordered, taking charge. Then he whacked the six-week-old infant on the back and grabbed a towel. The baby choked, gasped, then threw up into the towel, which John was holding under her mouth. She gasped and threw up again, but she began to breathe before she continued to choke. John turned the towel over and caught the undigested food again. She threw up five times, and each time John caught her vomit in the towel. As soon as he could, John dialed the operator and asked for help.

"There's a baby here that's been choking. She's breathing again, but we need an ambulance."

There was a pause. "You're making a prank call, right?" the operator's tin voice answered.

"No! No! There's a baby here—"

"What's your name, young man."

"My name? . . . a baby is choking . . . ah. My name is John Meranda."

"Where do you live?"

"No, you don't understand." John's knuckles turned white as he clasped the phone. "You need to send an ambulance here to this address."

"Your home address, please." He thought he heard her yawn.

John proceeded to answer all her questions. He told her he was a Boy Scout and that he had learned how to help a choking person. He told her his name, his address, his troop number, even his Scout ranking before she would believe him. Then he sent Troy and the baby's sister outside to flag down the ambulance and direct the crew to the right apartment when it arrived.

The baby's name was Ashley Griffin, and she was rushed to the children's hospital in Indianapolis, where a physician determined that she had had a seizure provoked by an intolerance to solid foods. The doctor said that if John had not run in and saved her, her death would have been reported as a Sudden Infant Death Syndrome (SIDS) incident. He prescribed a machine to monitor her breathing in the future.

John dropped by baby Ashley's home the next day to ask her parents how she was doing. Ashley was still in the hospital and would remain there for a week, but when her parents saw John, they grabbed and hugged him. The baby's mother cried and thanked John repeatedly for saving her baby's life.

John continued to drop in at Ashley's apartment to talk, along with all the other visits on his newspaper route. The experience didn't help him to improve his collection routine. He continued to secretly pay Leo's bills when he needed it, along with those of a few other senior citizens. He didn't tell his mom.

But John's small-town life didn't remain the same. Newspaper reporters from the *Lebanon Reporter, Indianapolis News,* and the *Indianapolis Star* visited him for interviews.

"What's the big deal?" he asked the reporters. "I think I was just doing my duty. I'm glad my parents kept after me to get merit badges. I couldn't usually catch someone's throw up. It would have make me sick. But, you know, I didn't even think about it." He smiled. "That's just what we're all here for. To do our duties. That's what my training in Boy Scouts was for."

Later in the evening, after the reporters had left, John sat with his parents on the front porch swing and shared his reaction with them. "You know, I pray all the time. I pray for health, and then I thank God for food and pretty much the usual stuff. But you know, I think it was the Holy Ghost that got me to see what was wrong behind that door. It really strengthened my testimony. Heavenly Father is really real, and he answers our prayers if we have faith in him."

It was a quiet Indiana evening, air soggy, crickets buzzing. The glinting stars reminded him of hundreds of animals' eyes in a dark forest. John liked animals. "I want to go on a mission someday, and then I want to be veterinarian or a horse jockey."

His dad leaned his head back in the swing and smiled. "That sounds about right. You like taking care of things, don't you—cats, horses, birds, bikes, lawns, old people, babies . . . " His voice droned on.

That was only the beginning of John's celebrity status. The State Bank of Lizton gave him a $100 savings bond, and the mayor gave him the key to the city.

Jason Smith's mom sent John's story to Chester Price in the Indianapolis Scout office. Chester sent it to national headquarters in Texas, and the national office conducted an investigation. The next thing John knew, he was standing at Camp Belzer in August, along Fall Creek near Indianapolis, watching Chester Price pin the Boy Scout Heroism Award on his tan Scout shirt. Big stuff.

Then the National Association of Mutual Insurance Companies awarded him the Distinguished Citizenship Award and flew John and his parents to San Francisco in September to receive it.

The biggest surprise came in February, when John was selected by the Boy Scouts of America as one of seven Scouts in the nation to deliver their Scouting report to President George Bush at the White House in Washington, D.C. They reported the achievements of the organization and Scouting goals for the future.

John shook the President's hand right there in the Roosevelt Room in the White House, next to the fireplace with the Peace Prize. President Bush looked big to John as he tilted his head upward and squeezed the President's hand. However, when President Bush heard John's story, John must have appeared pretty big to him too.

Tallee Billiard. Above, visiting at the Soldiers and Sailors Home.
Left, as president of S.A.D.D. (Students Against Drunk Driving).
Below, with poster she designed for C.A.R.E. (committed to awareness,
response, and education concerning substance abuse).

Peter Fellmann

REACHING OUT

PARENTS

Gary A. and Stasia J. Billiard

LOCATION OF STORY

Norwalk, Ohio

"There he is." Thirteen-year-old Tallee Billiard stood at the top of the wooden bleachers overlooking the Huron County Fair in Norwalk, Ohio, with her friends. A warm breeze brushed her neck and tangled her blond curls as she scrutinized the crowd for a certain boy she had seen. They had climbed the bleachers to gain a better view.

"I see him," Tina squealed, pointing toward a hot dog stand. "What a cute guy."

"How old do you think he is?" Angie asked. "Come on," she called over her shoulder as she scrambled down the concrete steps. "Hurry. Let's not let him get away."

The three girls began leaping down the steps with Angie in the lead. Halfway down, Tina, who was behind Tallee, tripped. She flailed her arms for something to grasp and banged into Tallee's back. The impact hurled Tallee through the air like a rag doll, down the fifteen remaining steps. She smacked the front of her head and then bashed the side of her skull against the cement when she hit the bottom of the stairs.

As Tallee lay sprawled and unconscious, her friends tried to revive her while two teenaged girls from a food concession stand ran to the administration office to call for an ambulance. The woman behind the counter glanced up over the rims of her glasses and said, "I'm sorry, sweeties, but you're not allowed to use this phone." She cracked her gum. "You'll have to go find the ambulance. It's somewhere here on the fairgrounds."

The girls' mouths fell open as they stared at each other. They couldn't believe her curt reply, but they turned and tore out the door. They needed help fast. They charged past a booth with hand-embroidered linens, past the ring toss, the Tilt-a-Whirl, the restrooms. They stopped to ask at a hamburger stand, but no one knew where the ambulance was.

They darted back to Tallee. An adult who had joined Tallee's friends told the girls to go back to the administration office again and tell them it was an emergency. One of the friends scribbled the Billiards' phone number on a scrap of paper and gave it to the two teenagers. The girls flew back and breathlessly repeated their story to the same woman. "It's an emergency!" they pleaded.

The same woman twirled her glasses in her hand. "Look, sweeties. I'm sorry. You're just not allowed to use this phone. Find the police booth. You can use their phone."

The girls stared at the woman with wide eyes, but they didn't take precious time to argue. They dashed out of the office and finally found the police booth. After calling for an ambulance, the girls phoned Tallee's parents. By the time an ambulance arrived on the scene, twenty minutes had passed since Tallee had fallen, and she had stopped breathing.

Tallee's parents reached the hospital in Norwalk seven

minutes ahead of the ambulance, and Tallee learned later from them exactly what had happened.

When she arrived on the stretcher, she was unconscious and convulsing. Both the front and back of her brain were bruised, and she had suffered a skull fracture and a broken wrist. The doctors in Norwalk didn't expect her to pull through.

Brother Billiard had recently joined the Church, and right there in the emergency room he placed his hands on his daughter's fractured head and gave her a blessing. Suddenly, Tallee's lifeless feet flopped over one another. It startled the nurse, who nervously giggled and said, "She acts like nothing is wrong." Brother and Sister Billiard looked at each other and nodded.

For five days Tallee lay unconscious while her family and friends prayed. When she finally awoke from the coma, she said, "I'm hungry. Can I have something to eat, please?"

Her father kissed her bandaged forehead. "It's like a rebirth," he said aloud. "Heavenly Father has given her back to us."

Tallee's parents hugged her carefully and wiped their eyes.

"What day is it?" Tallee asked.

"You've been unconscious for five days," her mother answered.

"Five days? I can't remember anything."

Her brother, Dirk, said, "No one expected you to live, kid." He plumped Tallee's pillows. "You should have seen yourself hooked up to all those tubes and wires."

Tallee stayed in the hospital for one more week. Before the accident, Tallee had earned straight A's at school. After the accident, she lost her memory of small things and struggled to concentrate on details. Her hand wobbled and caused her to write illegibly. She lost most of the eighth-grade basic principles of algebra and science. She would later have to study to fill in the gaps.

"I'm not great at anything," she confided to her mother as she huddled over her algebra book on the kitchen table. "I had wanted so much to be on the volleyball team, but I was in the hospital during the tryouts."

"Tallee, you're still getting good grades. That in itself is remarkable."

"But that's just because my teachers like me. I don't really deserve those grades."

"You can do other things to make a name for yourself at Norwalk," her mother said consolingly. "You're good at other things."

"No, I'm not. Dirk has his trombone. He's even played with the Cleveland Youth Orchestra. He gets good grades, and besides, he looks just like Tom Cruise. What more could he want?"

"You're five years younger. It takes some time to discover talents."

"I play the clarinet, but I'm not very great at it. I can't even write a sentence that's really readable. And the doctor won't let me ride horses anymore, or play ball, or skate—"

"Tallee, you have many talents." Her mother looked up at the ceiling. "Do you remember the trip we took to Guatemala? The rest of us walked past all those begging children because there were so many of them, but you stopped and shared all your gum with them."

Tallee smiled at the memory.

Her mother continued. "And I remember another time when you made me buy T-shirts from that poor old woman at the grocery store because you felt sorry for her."

"And I dressed my teddy bear in those shirts."

"What I'm trying to say is that you have always had

compassion for others, and that's probably the most important talent of all." Her mother leaned over and kissed the top of Tallee's head. "Give it time."

Tallee lay in bed one night, pulling up the sheet under her chin. She looked around her room at the picture of the Washington Temple on her wall, at the poster of Hamlet, and at the one of French author Emile Zola. A stack of books and plays sat on her dresser: *Jane Eyre,* Shakespeare's plays, and the Book of Mormon. Then she sat up and rubbed her fingers over a plaque of Elmer Fudd she had bought at a garage sale for only four dollars.

She smiled. This was her room. It had her mark on it, but there was nothing in it to show that she was someone special. She squeezed the sides of her temples. How long would she have to sit back and watch other people doing great things? She wanted to be popular or at least to do something special.

Then she prayed: "Father in Heaven, I have always believed the Church was true, ever since I was seven and went to the first meeting with my mom. I believe in prayer. Please help me do something special."

In the morning, she woke up thinking that maybe being popular wasn't so important. Ideas popped into her mind. There were lots of things she could accomplish.

She volunteered as a candy striper at the hospital, where she could bring water and snacks to patients and run errands. She also began stopping at the Old Soldiers' and Sailors' Home to visit an arthritic, seventy-year-old man in a wheelchair. Tallee watched his hands shake as he lifted a cup to his lips and stubbornly refused help. She understood that.

Tallee practiced long hours in the evenings trying to steady her own hands while completing homework. She prayed each night and wiped perspiration from her forehead in the day as she struggled with her wobbling pencil. Month after month, through the eighth and ninth grades, she progressed, the steadiness slowly returning. She painted her nails bright pink to practice fine motor control, while inside she still longed for something more to do.

She remembered how her father had struggled and agonized over giving up social drinking to join the church. It had been a difficult task for him, but two years later, he had been called to be bishop of the Sandusky Ward. Tallee thanked her Father in Heaven that her father had given up alcohol and that her family was pulling together, and it gave her an idea.

As a result, Tallee joined Students Against Drunk Drivers (SADD) at Norwalk High School and started to inform others about the dangers of drunk driving. Some of the students began to respect her for her beliefs. When she was elected president of SADD, she started a new program.

"I think we need a program for baby-sitters who sometimes get driven home by a parent who has been drinking," Tallee told her SADD committee.

"Right," a committee member said. "It's not safe for the sitter."

Tallee questioned, "I wonder if we could get high school students to drive them home?"

"Wow. What a cool idea."

Tallee made up a roster of the names and phone numbers of senior high school students who agreed to drive baby-sitters home from tending jobs if the sitters' employers ever returned home drunk. Because of limited funds, she distributed it only to sixth graders, but word spread quickly, and it proved to be a successful program.

When a local juvenile court judge, Thomas Heydinger, formed a community committee, consisting of community

members, churches, and two high school student representatives, to study the growing problem of delinquency
and substance abuse, Norwalk High School administra-
tors suggested that Tallee be a part of that committee.

While serving on the committee, Tallee designed a
poster discouraging substance abuse. Although she struggled over the poster, she thanked God that her hands had
become completely steady. She drew three trees of increas-
ing size with the caption, "Our substance abuse problem
is growing, but awareness isn't." The poster was repro-
duced and displayed in fifteen different stores and public
buildings.

At the Halloween hayrides, she organized an information booth stocked with pamphlets against substance
abuse to be handed out to youth, and she began giving
speeches in the community on behalf of SADD to other
young people and even to parents.

Tallee's reputation for fighting substance abuse spread
through the high school, and she influenced other students. For example, one evening at a party, someone
asked her, if she wanted a drink. From the other room, a
guy yelled, "Don't ask her. She's a Mormon, and she
doesn't drink."

"Don't push her," another boy said. "If she drank anything . . . Well, I'd be . . . sort of disappointed."

At a beach party one of the most popular girls came up
to Tallee and asked, "Would you be disappointed in me if
I drank?"

Tallee answered, "You have the right to choose what
you want to do. Everyone has that freedom." The girl
smiled, and Tallee couldn't help but notice that her friend
didn't drink all that night. With Tallee's encouragement,
two young men also stopped drinking completely.

Besides gaining the ability to influence those about
her to avoid alcohol, Tallee discovered that she also had

special acting talent, and she participated in several dramas, some at the Cleveland Playhouse.

One summer, Tallee went to Villennes, France, for one month as a foreign exchange student. The first night, she attended a yard party with some students who were celebrating passing a major exam. A few parents and even some teachers were there. They surrounded Tallee and tried to encourage her to taste the wine.

"Try some of this wine. It is the best in the world."

"No, thank you," Tallee struggled with French. "I like the juice, please."

"A little wine is good for you. It aids the digestion."

"It's the water that is unhealthful." They all laughed.

She looked around the table at their smiling faces and felt strange with her glass of orange juice. Fearful that she was offending them, she wondered if she should pretend to drink some of the wine. It was so hard to explain in French.

"Here try this, my dear. This is the best of the vine."

Tallee wondered if she could keep saying "no" anymore. She silently prayed that she could be strong, and then almost miraculously, they quit asking her. This happened several times. Each time that Tallee felt herself weakening under the pressure, she prayed for strength, and they quit asking her to take a drink.

That night she got on her knees and thanked her Father in Heaven that he hadn't let her be tested beyond what she was capable of handling. "I realize now, Father, that when I'm trying to do what is right, you will protect me. You can help me overcome anything I need to. You have helped me regain my hands and have shown me how I can serve with them."

Despite asthma, allergy, and back problems, Alan Barlow continued to excel in hurdles and basketball

Alan Barlow, #33

ALAN BARLOW

JUMPING HURDLES

PARENTS

Ronald K. and Sarah Barlow

LOCATION OF STORY

Montezuma Creek, Utah

Alan sat cross-legged on the roof of White Horse High School. He sniffed and wiped his muscled arm over puffy eyes. It was good to be alone. He had to think. Out on the compound he watched people gathering in clusters. They would be talking about Steward, trying to understand.

In the distance Alan saw an oil truck filling up next to one of the giant silver tanks. The oil rigs on the Navajo Reservation in Montezuma Creek in Southern Utah reminded him of giant praying mantises pumping their heads up and down, sipping up oil. Life cranked on.

He had to make sense of things. When had he first been aware of his own sickness or of Steward's kindness? He had been the sick one, while Steward had always been so hardy. It didn't make sense, but he did know their lives had woven together like two colors of wool yarn in one of his mother's Navajo rugs, and the threads involved friendship, sports, and his constant fight with sickness.

His memories flashed by like sheet lightning.

He could see himself, nine years old and racing out the door of Montezuma Creek Elementary. He had loved recess, and that day they would race around the dirt field to see who was the fastest. Alan's long legs were bent in a V, ready to catapult him to the lead, and he almost always won.

Steward Sam stood next to him. "Today I win," he teased.

Alan grinned, for he knew he could run faster than Steward.

"Ready. Go!" Mrs. Eck yelled.

As he leaped in front of his classmates, his tennis shoes puffed up sprays of dust. Halfway across the field, it happened. He began to cough, and his windpipe seemed to narrow.

"My friend," Steward called out as he pulled along beside him, "what's the matter?"

Alan slowed down, coughed, choked, and thought he would die right there, but he stumbled ahead and crossed the finish line in the middle of the pack. Steward was right with him all the time.

That was the first episode, but from then on, every time Alan caught a cold, a sore throat, or any other illness, the wheezing slipped in on the tail of his sickness. Sometimes when he and Steward played tag at school, darting through green yucca plants, the tightness grabbed his chest.

Finally, Alan's parents took him to an allergist, 120 miles away in Durango, Colorado, and he learned he had asthma. He was allergic to his cat, horses, dogs, anything furry, dust, molds, and practically every plant that grew in Montezuma Creek. Even changes of weather or exercise could trigger an asthmatic attack. The doctor started him on allergy shots to build up his resistance and prescribed several types of medication.

"My peace pipe," Alan often said, laughing and patting the inhaler in his pocket.

Alan's family lived on the compound for school teachers because his dad was principal of White Horse High School. Their home had a bathroom and kitchen appliances, unlike the homes of eighty percent of the children from outlying areas who didn't have running water or phones. Most of the students lived in one-story wood, brick, or tile houses with two or three rooms, like his friend, Steward. Some students still lived in dirt hogans.

Although bouts of poor health remained a problem for Alan, he didn't have another serious asthma attack until his sophomore year at high school, during a junior varsity basketball game with their arch rivals, the Monticello Buckaroos. He was only one of four guys who hadn't fouled out in the fourth quarter.

"We're down forty points. Come on, you guys," Alan urged.

"We've already lost," a teammate moaned.

Another said, "Let's just get it over with."

Angry at his teammates, Alan exploded with energy, darting, jumping for rebounds, and stealing the ball mid-pass from his opponents. Although Alan had usually been known as the jumper who captured rebounds, he now gritted his teeth and scored eight points for his team in the fourth quarter. He saw Steward standing on the sideline, grinning at him and punching his fist in the air. They lost, but Alan had learned that he could score.

Excited and heated up, he didn't feel it coming. As Alan headed back to the locker room, he stopped in the hallway where his coach was lecturing the boys. Suddenly Alan's vision grew wavy, and the coach's voice sounded tunneled and far away. Alan's windpipe slammed shut like a steel trap. He stopped breathing, his knees buckled beneath him, and he collapsed to the floor.

When he regained consciousness, people blurred before his eyes. His dad kneeled over him, rubbing his hands, his muscles. His mom's smile floated above his face. "*Shiyaazh,* my son. *T'aa ako,* it's okay." She held his inhaler to his mouth, but because his chest was so contracted, he couldn't suck in the medication.

"Help me, Father," he prayed in his mind.

He heard his teammates' and parents' voices:

"He's cold."

"Grab a blanket."

"His muscles are frozen up tight. Look, I can't even bend his arm."

His dad's calm face reassured him, and he began to relax. He tried the inhaler again, and this time some medication blew into his lungs so that he could begin to breathe again. He refused to go to the hospital in Monticello but instead stayed to watch the next game.

What he remembered most from that game, however, was that Steward had seen him play and must have respected him. Steward's stocky body made him the top wrestler and the hardest hitter on the football team, and he was also president of the sophomore class. He had been elected president practically every year up to this time, except as a freshman, when Alan was president.

Steward didn't always respect him. One afternoon during a football game, Steward tore into him. Alan was one of the escorts for a homecoming princess at the halftime, but he didn't want people to think he liked this girl, so he just hid in the school hall.

Steward had stamped into the hall, wearing oversized football pads that made his shoulders look even broader than usual. Sweat and black mud were smeared under his eyes.

"Do you know I just left the team in the locker room and escorted *your* princess onto the field?" He pointed at him. "You were supposed to do that, and you're here hanging out in the halls?"

"But I didn't want anyone to think I liked her," Alan protested.

"Well, guess what?" Steward placed his hands on his hips. "I didn't want anyone to think I liked her, either." He turned and marched back to score fourteen points in the game.

Alan felt like a coyote, the creature that caused much of the evil in Navajo legends. Alan was usually the one who always helped other students with homework, who complimented teammates, who comforted his friends. So how could he have been so stupid?

When he needed Steward, his friend always managed to be around. Once, as Alan left the locker room after a basketball game, some players from the defeated team challenged him to a fight.

"Look, we don't need to fight. Let's just go our separate ways," Alan tried to reason. There were three of them, and Alan didn't like fighting anyway.

"Let's see if you're as hot off the court as you are on." The three boys took fighting stances, legs spread apart.

Suddenly Steward appeared behind him, along with a few other teammates. "You can take my word for it. He's an okay guy, and you can leave him alone," Steward said quietly. "Because if you don't, he won't be the only one you'll fight."

The three boys looked at each other, stuttered some excuses, and left.

Another time Alan helped Steward, but in a different way. He found his friend in front of the gym door, smoking with some other guys. Alan knew Steward respected his Mormon beliefs, so he called Steward over and asked, "What are you doing?"

Steward grinned and tilted his head back to look up at

Alan, trying to hide his cigarette behind his back. But the puffs drifted upward like smoke signals. "What does it look like I'm doing?"

"Don't be smart with me. You know better than that." Steward looked down, then away.

"Besides," Alan said as he laughed, "you know what that does to my asthma."

Steward chuckled. "Okay, okay. I'll put it out." He dropped the cigarette and kicked dirt over it with the toe of his wrestling shoe. "Are you happy now?"

"Yes, I'm happy."

"Now go back to the game," Steward commanded.

"All right, but why don't you pass that advice on to the rest of those friends. Tell them to put their cigarettes out, too."

Steward shook his head and grinned. "Okay, okay." He held his palms up and backed away. "All right, you win."

Alan never saw him smoke after that. He also invited Steward to attend seminary, and they sometimes discussed their different beliefs, but Steward was steeped in Navajo traditions. He had a hogan and sweat house in his backyard, where he'd place fire-hot rocks and pour water over them in order to sit in the steaming heat, to cleanse his body and mind and to renew his connections with the Great Spirit. He always wore a beaded Navajo cedar-berry necklace for luck.

Alan attended seminary without Steward in the early morning and began reading the Book of Mormon and the Bible each day. He was only one of twenty Mormons in a school with 230 kids. Although drinking alcohol caused problems for many youths and their parents on the reservation, no one pressured him to try anything, partly because they knew that his dad was in the bishopric and that both his parents had served missions, and partly because they knew he wouldn't do it.

Alan talked to other friends about the Church, like his first girlfriend, Shannon, who asked him many questions, started attending seminary, and who got baptized at the end of his senior year.

Another student, Tommy, asked him how he could be so happy when he kept having health problems. Alan told him it was because of the Holy Ghost and explained a little about the Church. They had several discussions, but Tommy's parents would not allow the missionaries to come to his house, and shortly after, Tommy moved to Oklahoma and Alan lost contact with him.

Alan continued to have health problems. Besides asthma, he injured his knee in track and had to sit out the football season, watching Steward tear up the field without him. Then he slipped some disks in his back and also developed Bell's palsy, or paralysis on the right side of his face, and he had to spend several weeks on his back on his bedroom floor to recuperate from both.

Once as he lay on the floor staring up at the ceiling, he asked his mother, "Why does my body constantly do these things? Steward never gets sick or injured." He glanced at his sports hats gathering dust on his shelves and hanging from the walls. He felt as if he too were collecting dust just lying there on the floor.

His mother kneeled beside him and stroked his hair. "Do you remember the story of the Long Walk of the Navajo from Fort Defiance, Arizona, to Fort Sumner in New Mexico?"

"Sort of."

"Remember great-grandmother, Asdzaan Nez, the tall woman. She was pregnant and had her baby on the trail. Then she had to forage for wild onions and berries, and she even ate lizards and mice to keep alive, but she was wise and saved her four sheep on the trip home instead of eating them as many others did. When she got to the end of the trail and started her new home, she was able to develop a big herd."

His father stood in the doorway, listening to the familiar story and added, "And your struggles are storing up, just like letting the sheep reproduce, and someday all these struggles will pay off in strength and wisdom."

"I know," Alan whispered. "I'm probably really lucky I've been able to play sports at all."

Back in school, eager to play basketball, he set his jaw and promised himself he wouldn't let asthma, knees, back, or anything else interfere with the rest of this last season. He banged his locker shut with a fist, then stooped over the fountain for a drink of water.

Steward called him over to his locker. He always seemed to sense the right moments. "I've got something for you," he said and handed Alan a cedar-berry necklace, like the one Steward wore.

Alan fingered the blue beads and light brown berries.

"It wards off the *Chinde,* the evil ones, and will bring you good luck," but there was no laughter in Steward's voice. "You need it." Steward looked Alan straight in the eye, his brows knitted together.

"Thanks," Alan said softly. He placed the necklace over his head and rubbed the smooth beads as he watched Steward trot off with his ponytail bouncing at the back of his head.

As captain of the varsity team, Alan finished the basketball season, their team winning two-thirds of the games. And at the state track meet, he managed to score second place in the 110 hurdles in spite of his old knee injury.

He accomplished more than that. Using old missionary lessons as a guide, he helped to develop a curriculum for teaching the Navajo language in school. He also excelled in band and drama and won math and science awards.

While his senior year flashed by, he knew he also needed to practice for the Sterling Scholar competition in the spring, the state competition for scholars. With a 3.9 grade point average, he was hoping to do well in that.

One cold, spring evening when he thought he had his asthma under better control, he was jogging home from Ginger's house next door. Suddenly his lungs constricted, and his muscles froze. He collapsed on the gravel and gasped for breath, terrified because it was dark except for light from the stars, and no one was out on the street.

He prayed, "Father in Heaven, help me. Send someone to help me."

Some little kids wandered by, but they must have thought he was playing because Alan couldn't call out for help. He fought the sensation that he was passing out, and again he prayed.

Immediately Ginger came out of her house, saw him lying there, and ran to get his father.

His dad and the neighbors lifted him onto a wool blanket and carried him to the living-room floor. Alan's dad gave him a priesthood blessing, and as soon as he finished, Alan's airway opened up for a second, long enough for his dad to spray his inhaler and get the medicine into his lungs.

Alan stayed all night on the floor with a blanket over him, and he didn't feel angry. He just lay there and thought of his great-grandmother, Asdzaan Nez, foraging for wild onions and eating mice to keep the baby alive inside her stomach—his grandfather. He prayed a silent prayer of thanks to God for the priesthood and for sending Ginger out of her house that cold night.

It was Ginger who brought him the terrible news of Steward. Alan was gathering his scholarship papers, which he needed to give to the counselor the following morning. He hoped for a good scholarship to pay for college, and he planned to put in one year of school before his mission.

Ginger walked into his house with a girlfriend. He looked up, startled at Ginger's clouded eyes. "It's Steward," she said and sucked in her lips. "He was in a car accident just a little while ago." She paused, then added, "He's dead, Alan."

Alan shook his head slowly. "No! It has to be someone else. Steward is always so careful. He never gets sick or anything. He's always around."

"It was him, Alan. It was."

He held up his hand in protest, while his voice rose. "Why do you say this? You come in here and say terrible things like this." Even as he spoke, his scalp tingled, and his lungs tightened. He grabbed his chest and felt as if he were suffocating as he backed toward his bedroom. "No! It isn't true. This isn't funny." His knees weakened beneath him, and he folded on his bed. A loud cry burst from his chest. "Noooo!"

Ginger patted his back.

"This is too much. How can he die? What am I going to do?" he sobbed. "This is like walking with one leg. How can Steward die? Everyone loves him."

Slowly Ginger told the story. Steward and some friends had been driving home from a powwow in Albuquerque, New Mexico. They had all fallen asleep, including the driver, and the car had run off the road and rolled once.

Immediately following the accident, Steward had walked around with a small trickle of blood oozing from his mouth, but he had acted coherent and even tried to help. When the ambulance arrived, the medics had made Steward lie down on a stretcher on his back, even though he appeared stable, while they took care of the other kids. When they returned to check Steward, they could find no pulse. He had simply passed away unnoticed on the stretcher. One other boy died and another was hospitalized, while the fourth boy survived with less serious injuries.

Alan lay on his bed and cried for three hours until his swollen cheeks puffed under his eyes. He had to leave to sort out his thoughts. He walked for a while, tumbleweeds scratching his ankles, but he didn't even kick them away. Then he climbed on top of the high school roof.

Alan stared across the sandy mesa. The sun would soon slice through the hills bunched against the eastern horizon. He had spent most of the night thinking, reliving his friendship with Steward. He knelt there on the roof and prayed to understand what had happened.

A small voice seemed to whisper to him: "Why are you feeling sad? Why are you worrying about yourself? You know more about the plan of salvation that most of the people in high school, and you know you'll see him again. Tomorrow you must go back to help the others because they don't understand our Father's plan."

The next day Alan walked the silent hallways of the school, hallways that usually jostled with kids sharing books, shouting insults, tossing crumbled papers. Now as his friends passed by with downcast eyes, he heard only the thud of shoes.

"Remember the good times," he said in a weak voice to his friends. "Remember how he used to make us laugh." Alan's voice gained strength. "Do you really think that he is gone forever? He's only gone from us physically.

You're going to see him again." The students listened to
Alan, and he comforted them.

Shortly after Steward's death, the school retired his
football jersey, number 21.

With slightly swollen eyes and without advance practice, Alan attended the Sterling Scholar competition in
Green River, but he prayed before he left. He told the
judges that White Horse High was not a bad school and
that he was happy to be attending there. He told them
that he planned to go on a mission, was proud to be a
Mormon, and was grateful for the strength it gave him:
strength to excel, to face sickness and even the death of
his best friend.

Without the necessary preparation, he was awarded
runner-up in the general scholarship category, and on
March 6, as number one in the state, he received Gov-
ernor Norman Bangerter's Ethnic Young Achiever's Award.

Back home, Alan boxed his seventy baseball caps to
make room for his trophies. He placed Steward's picture
next to his Eagle Scout Award. For some reason he
remembered Steward standing in the school hall in the
autumn, refusing the chance to be president of the school.
"Give someone else a chance," he had said.

Alan hoped he had helped Steward too, and maybe
his friend would remember their gospel discussions and
accept the gospel in the spirit world. He liked to think so.
He knew that he didn't understand everything yet but
that sometime this would all make sense, like the four
sheep of Asdzaan Nez.

A bright ray of sunshine bounced from his state track
medal. From now on he would have to jump hurdles without Steward, but he knew Steward's wisdom would
always be there for him as long as Alan could remember
him.

Charlene Ahn at age eight (left) and age fourteen (above), after winning different state music competitions

Charlene, age three, reading out loud at her nursery school

CHARLENE AHN

IT'S NOT ALWAYS EASY BEING A "BRAIN"

PARENTS

John and Sonia Ahn

LOCATION OF STORY

Kinston, North Carolina

The boys and girls in the Sunday School class for fifteen-year-olds sat mystified in their folding chairs and spouted Book of Mormon questions at tiny, five-year-old Charlene Ahn. The youth in the Kinston Second Ward in Kinston, North Carolina, floundered for more difficult questions to stump Charlene.

"Okay, I've got one," said a girl snuggled in a mohair sweater. Her elbows were balanced on her knees, and her chin was cupped in the palms of her hands. "What was the name of the person who tried to destroy the church and who had a famous father who—"

"Alma, Alma the Younger." Charlene rubbed her shiny patent-leather shoe down the leg of her tights.

"What was the name of the people who came before the Nephites and Laman—"

"Jaredites." Charlene gazed out the window, as though bored.

"How many times have you read the Bible?"

Since Charlene had comprehensive children's versions of the scriptures, she blurted out, "Probly ten times!"

The girl in the mohair whistled. "I've never met a five-year-old before who made me feel inadequate."

"Me neither."

"I want to ask you something," a boy said. "I want to know what you want to be when you grow up."

Charlene scrunched her nose and gazed toward the ceiling. "I want to be . . . mmm . . . maybe an astronaut, but I like artists too—I want to be a waitress at Pizza Hut."

The roar of laughter could be heard clear down the hall.

As far back as Charlene could remember, she could read. Her mother and father read to her often as a baby. By age two and a half, she could read all the signs at the grocery store.

One spring day, when Charlene was nearly three, her mother arrived to pick her up from nursery school. Charlene watched her mother's mouth drop open as Charlene sat propped on a stool, her broom-thin legs swinging beneath her, reading *Betsy's Birthday* to the class. She saw the pride in her mother's eyes and knew she had pleased her, and she thought everyone else would feel the same way about her talents.

Nothing appeared too hard for Charlene to learn. Aunt Mary Pak, a concert pianist, sent her a small Suzuki violin for her third birthday, and Charlene began taking lessons on the scaled down, one-tenth-sized violin. Before long she was mastering two violin books a year, while the average student attempted only one book.

Her mother called out the fingering and bowing and sang each note, while Charlene stood slightly knocked kneed in front of the music stand and sawed back and forth. Charlene's perfect pitch helped her match the tones easily.

At age five she began picking out familiar tunes with two fingers on the piano. "I want to play the piano," she announced.

"You already play the violin, and I think that might be too much." She felt her mother's hands stroking fingers through her hair.

"Please. I want to," she begged. "Please."

Her mother relented, and Charlene began playing their Kimball upright piano forty-five minutes a day along with her regular hour on the violin.

When she turned six, her violin teacher, JoAnne Bath, took her, the youngest student, with the other Suzuki violinists of Eastern North Carolina on a performing tour to Great Britain. Charlene performed in small country churches and larger city churches with tall Gothic arches.

As Charlene grew older, her mother would shake her head and say, "You know, you amaze me."

Charlene beamed, expecting a compliment.

"You are so bright. You always bring me home papers with 100s on the top."

"I know. I bring you home boring scores."

"But you forget you're cooking something and burn up my pans, and you constantly lose things."

Charlene blushed.

"Most of the time, the things you lose are just in your bedroom, buried under piles of socks and T-shirts . . ."

"I know. I know. I just don't remember where I've put . . ."

Her mother interrupted, "But the amazing thing is that you never seem to lose a book, even though they're stacked everywhere—on your dresser, on the floor, under the bed. Explain that to me." Her mother laughed.

Charlene shrugged her shoulders. "I like books." She

even buried her nose into the pages of their encyclopedias, carrying the books before her like a mask as she went to the bathroom to take a shower and accidentally smacked into walls. She would usually beg her dad, who was a chemical engineer at DuPont, to take her every Saturday to the Lenoir County Public Library, where he waited all day for her to read and study.

She loved her music the most, though. When she was eight, she won the Winston-Salem Symphony Orchestra's Youth Talent Search by playing Vivaldi's Violin Concerto in A Minor flawlessly. She won it again when she was twelve with Bruch's Violin Concerto No. 1 in G Minor, and her little sister, Christina, won in the ten and under group at the same time.

Because Charlene devoted so much time to music and academic studies, she excelled in both, but she didn't feel so successful with friendships in grade school. Although other children liked to sit by her to get answers, Charlene didn't quite know what to say to them and found their interests growing further and further apart. Her girlfriends talked about Barbie dolls and cartoons, but they squinted their eyes at her when she shoved her round glasses up the ridge of her nose and tried to teach them how to balance an equation.

Her teacher in the gifted class in sixth grade handed her an algebra and a geometry book. "I can't teach you anything, Charlene. Here, read these."

Charlene pored over the books and often stayed in at recess to devour the pages of polynomials and geometric theorems, but she watched wistfully as the other girls chased each other out to recess.

Sometimes a girl would call to her, "Come on out, Charlene."

"I'm coming," she'd answer. Her heart would race as she followed and listened to them talk.

"Did you see TV last night?"

"Nancy is having a pizza party, and she's inviting boys."

"Look, my sister glued on my nails."

"Oh, where'd you get them?"

Charlene often followed behind until she found herself squeezed out and leaning against the brick wall of the school. She didn't know what to say or how to enter into these strange conversations. It would have been easier for her to speak French.

"Father in heaven," she would pray, "why am I so different? Is it just because I'm smart? Maybe I should pretend to be stupid." But even as she said it, she knew it would be like wearing a Halloween mask all the time, and it wouldn't be right. "Help me to find a friend," she'd finish.

Though her dad tried hard to develop her physical skills to make her well-rounded, she didn't enjoy the swimming, skating, or gymnastic lessons. When kids threw the ball at her, she often dropped it. It stung her hands, and besides, her violin teacher constantly told her, "Be careful playing sports. You might break your finger and not be able to play the violin."

It offered a good excuse. Moreover, she thought sports were dumb. She couldn't see any reason for them at all.

However, her father said, "Charlene, we are so proud of you." He patted the music stand. "You are very intelligent both in school and music, and you are a very good girl who always does what our Father in Heaven would want you to do. Those are the most important things." He paused as he bent over and removed his shoes. Charlene knew he was working up to the punch line.

"You need to develop physically too," he continued. "It's important for your physical health to exercise." He smiled and punched his fist into his hand. "A sport like tennis would be fine. You could play it your whole life."

"I don't want to play tennis. Mrs. Bath tells me if I play sports, I'll break my finger and won't be able to play the violin."

"No, you won't. Don't worry about that."

She argued, but in the end she agreed. "But you'll be sorry if I break a finger," she warned.

At the beginning of seventh grade, the school super-intendent insisted that Charlene be tested to determine just where to place her. Although she hadn't taken the courses, she scored ninety-five percent in both algebra and geometry. The superintendent made arrangements for Charlene to attend middle school in the morning and high school in the afternoon for advanced biology, French, and algebra II. A teacher drove her to the high school each day.

Charlene didn't know the students there. She grew more lonely than ever and often passed down the hall without speaking to anyone.

"It doesn't help, Charlene, if you don't look at people and speak to them," her mother tried to console her after school.

"I'd speak to them, if they'd pay any attention to me," she cried into the palms of her hands. "I wish I weren't so different. I wish I were more like them."

Her mother rubbed her back. "Honey, God has given you special talents, and you've put years of your life into developing them. Everyone has special gifts that some-times make them feel lonely, but the answer isn't to behave like an 'ugly duckling.'" Her mother paused, then added, "You'll never be happy pretending you're a duck if you're a swan."

Charlene added, " . . . or an egret, or an emu, a dove,

a pigeon, a cygnet, a petrel, a heron, a limpkin, a wood-pecker, or even a duck-billed platypus," and she started to laugh.

Her mother chuckled and added, "If you are friend-lier, people will pay more attention to you."

"I am friendly, sort of."

"Honey, I've seen you. Sometimes you're so busy think-ing about a math puzzle that you don't even look at any-one. Sometimes you forget to eat."

"But . . . but sometimes that's because I don't have anyone to sit with in the lunchroom." Charlene wiped a tissue over her nose.

"Charlene, you have an exciting brain and don't always notice things around you." She laughed.

It didn't change anything, but it made her feel better about herself just to talk to her mother.

So Charlene spent a great deal of time with her little sister, Christina, who also loved books and music, and even though Christina was four years younger, she loved to hear about solving math puzzles. They played duets on their violins and rolled over the living room carpet in tickle fights.

At high school, Charlene tried harder to make friends, but the other girls talked about dating boys, listened to rock music, and wore name-brand clothes, while Charlene played music by Tchaikovsky and Schumann and some-times arrived at school in mismatched socks.

She thought books might make a safer topic. "Do you like to read books?" she asked Camille one day in her high school advanced biology class.

"Oh, yeah. Have you read the latest *Sweet Valley High* book?" She shoved it in Charlene's face.

"*Sweet Valley High?*" Charlene rooted frantically through her backpack. "Have you read this? It's one of the greatest American novels." She pulled out *The Scarlet Letter.*

Camille stared at her, shrugged her shoulders, and turned to speak to the girl behind her. Charlene was squeezed out again. This is impossible, she thought, like mixing oil and water.

When she arrived home, she pounded out her anger on the piano with the loud chords of Schumann's "Knight Ruppert." Then she picked up her violin and played Mendelssohn's Concerto in E Minor. The pensive melody drained away her depression, and she knew she was more comfortable with Mendelssohn than Camille.

Duke University conducted a Talent Identification Program search to find students with the highest scores on a Scholastic Aptitude Test normally given to high school students. At thirteen years of age, Charlene scored 770 out of 800 on both sections of the test. She achieved the highest SAT score in North Carolina and the second highest score of all 55,000 talented seventh graders who participated throughout sixteen states.

Charlene skipped the eighth grade entirely and began attending high school full time. Although this stimulated her academically, her social life suffered even more. At least at the middle school, she had attended with the kids she had known since grade school.

Thanks to her dad's persistence, she made the high school tennis team and won the award for most improved player. She began early morning seminary at six-thirty each morning and continued reading her scriptures each day—this time in French.

She won creative writing contests, geography bees, science competitions. She also became the cornerstone of the Quiz Bowl Team, which competed with other high schools in academic competitions. She gave a copy of the

Book of Mormon to a team member who grew curious over Charlene's ability to answer all the Quiz Bowl questions on religion.

Then one day in gym class it finally happened. It was a mixed class, and the sport of the day was football. A boy threw a nicely spiraling pass at Charlene, but as she caught it, her smallest finger on her left hand bent backward.

She didn't hear anything pop, and since her hand stung also, she really didn't notice the finger so much, which was only slightly swollen by the end of the school day. Later that night when she tried to play her violin, a burning pain seared through her finger, and she knew then that something was wrong.

The X-ray proved that she had chipped a piece of the bone off her little finger, and the doctor clamped it into a splint that prevented her from practicing the violin or piano.

"I'll bet you're excited," Camille said the next day in class. "Now you don't have to play football or even practice your violin anymore."

"Are you kidding? I'm devastated," Charlene moaned. "I love to practice."

Camille stared at her and then turned away.

As a result of her injury, Charlene couldn't play her instruments for four months, two months with her finger in a cast, and two more months for it to regain movement. Worse still, the injury prevented her from competing in the regional violin competition in Alabama, after she had won first place for all of North Carolina in the Music Teachers Association competition.

She tried desperately to learn new selections by listening to them on tape as the Suzuki method of instruction required, but she grew frustrated with analyzing, and her fingers ached to try the notes on her violin. She wondered if she would ever compete again.

That spring, after Charlene finally got the splint removed and began practicing her violin, she received the biggest surprise yet. A letter arrived in the mail inviting her to attend the Salute to Excellence Weekend, sponsored by the American Academy of Achievement. So Charlene and her parents flew to Las Vegas in June, where she was honored with fifty of the brightest and most successful adult leaders and 450 outstanding honor students from the fifty states.

She saw and listened to a host of famous people at the workshops and banquets, including Kevin Costner, Dolly Parton, Herschel Walker, William Sessions, General Norman Schwarzkopf, Steven Spielberg, and a host of other celebrities from business, science, entertainment, sports, arts, and politics.

At the black-tie banquet on Saturday evening, fifteen students were honored with the Golden Plate Award for being the most accomplished students in the United States. Charlene's face flushed, and she lowered her eyes when she heard her name announced as one of the fifteen winners.

Back in North Carolina, Charlene's teachers and her parents thought she needed a greater challenge than the regular schools could provide. She agreed reluctantly, and in the fall, she prepared to attend the North Carolina School of Science and Mathematics, a state residential public school that enrolled students with high aptitude and interest in scientific and mathematical studies and that ranked second in the nation for the most national merit finalists.

"But what if no one talks to me?" Charlene confided in her mother. "I can't even come home to talk to Christina except on long weekends."

"I know, sweetheart, and we're going to miss you around here too."

Charlene added, "What really worries me is that I might not find any friends, and I'll be even lonelier than ever."

"I'm sure you'll find friends," her mother consoled her. "I'm more worried that you'll put your shirt on backwards and forget your socks."

Charlene laughed.

Although her new school proved difficult academically, for the first time in her life she met other students who competed against her for grades. These same students loved to discuss Shakespeare and the ways to calculate integrals, and Charlene thought she was in heaven. She joined the tennis team (which practiced three hours each day), the chorus, the math and debate teams, and she donated three hours of service a week in the math department.

Excited and enthusiastic, Charlene found many new friends, including her roommate, Kathy, who also played the violin. They often talked for hours into the night from their bunk beds.

One night, Charlene decided to trust Kathy. "Do you sometimes forget things and not notice certain details? My mom sometimes calls me 'the absentminded professor.'"

"Yes, I do, sometimes," came the yawning reply.

They could hear the clock tick away for a minute. Then Kathy broke the silence. "Do you remember that velocity experiment in physics?" she asked. "I never did figure it out."

"You mean when we shot water balloons in the air to estimate initial velocity?"

"Yeah, I got soaked," Kathy chuckled. "My partner and I were standing too far apart."

"That's funny," Charlene added. "My partner and I had the same problem."

They both leaned up on their elbows and stared at each other across the darkened room. A slit of window light caught Kathy's shining teeth. She pointed at Charlene. "I can't believe it. It was you. You were my partner, and we didn't even remember."

Charlene squinted her eyes and answered, "You're right."

Laughter tumbled from Kathy's throat.

"You're as absentminded as I am," Charlene chuckled. "I didn't even remember it was you."

"My mom says I'm semiconscious," Kathy said and laughed again.

They giggled into the night, sharing absentminded stories, and in spite of the fact that Charlene felt homesick for her family, she nestled comfortably under the blankets at the School of Science and Math. It was okay to be different, and she was glad she had dedicated so many years to music and studies. She thanked her Father in Heaven for her talents, for parents who had supported her and raised her in the gospel, and for Kathy and her other friends who had similar interests. It was if she had finally come home.

Top, Harvey Calfrobe, age 4 1/2, with dog Mitch.
Right, Harvey with Queen's Venturer Award.
Bottom, Harvey enjoying one of his favorite pastimes.

HARVEY CALFROBE

COURAGE TO WIN

PARENTS
Harvey Cutter and Christina Calfrobe (deceased)

LOCATION OF STORY
Alberta, Canada

Harvey was born on a reservation in Southern Alberta, Canada, a member of the Blood Tribe. But he lived with the Blackfoot Tribe with his father and six brothers and sisters. His mother died of a drug and alcohol overdose before he entered school.

As an infant and young child, Harvey caught every cold and infection that came along, and often his cough seemed to last for months. As recovering from illnesses became more and more difficult, he grew steadily weaker, until one day when he was four years old, he could not summon the energy to get off his bed. He only wanted to lie there forever. A family member grew worried, called an ambulance, and Harvey was rushed to the Foothills Hospital in Calgary. After a series of blood tests, he was diagnosed as having acute lymphocytic leukemia, or cancer of the blood, and placed in the pediatric ontology unit. Doctors gave him no more than three years to live.

The Alberta Social Services quickly contacted Richard Thompson, a member of the Calgary West Stake, to ask if he and his wife, Susan, would accept Harvey as a foster child. Transporting Harvey from the reservation to his daily medical treatments would be impossible for Harvey's family. Although Richard and Susan had four children of their own, they agreed to accept Harvey into their home.

Susan drove Harvey to frequent treatments. With quiet acceptance, Harvey endured radiation, spinal taps, bone marrow tests, lumbar punctures, and all the other needle punctures and probes. He suffered through chemotherapy sessions sometimes five days at a time for three years.

Harvey smiled at Susan gratefully, displaying teeth that appeared oversized in his sunken cheeks. He surprised doctors when his cancer stopped spreading and went into remission only three months after he had arrived at the Thompson's home.

The Thompson children—Kristine, Kathie, Joanne, and Christopher—planned a birthday party for Harvey to celebrate his fifth birthday, but when they handed him colorfully wrapped gifts, he only stared at them.

"Go on, Harvey, open them," Kristine coaxed.

Harvey sat still on the couch and smiled.

"Why doesn't he open them?"

"Maybe he's never received a gift that was wrapped before," Susan suggested.

Kathie showed him how to tear off the ribbon and paper, and then Harvey really grinned.

Although Harvey's leukemia stayed in remission, life wasn't easy for him. He caught many infections that required hospital care, and it happened often on family vacations. When Harvey was five years old, he interrupted the family holiday by contracting a severe sore throat and developing a 104-degree temperature. He had to be flown from Okanogan Lake in British Columbia to the Foothills Hospital, and the same thing happened the next summer when he was six years old.

On the third attempted summer vacation at Shuswap Lakes, Harvey was able to stay at the resort and get better on antibiotics. He scurried across the beach like a brown squirrel, chasing his sisters, building sand castles, and playing catch with a two-foot beach ball. He kicked up sand, tumbled, caught water spray in his mouth, and even waded into the warm lake, and he didn't have to go to a hospital.

Harvey struggled at school, and as he looked at the strange little symbols on paper, he didn't understand their meanings or what his teacher was trying to tell him. He didn't understand why other children could learn so quickly and why it was so hard for him. Finally, Harvey was told he had a learning disability. That was okay, Harvey thought, because he had learned to be patient and to wait for good things.

Because he always smiled, said "Thank you," picked up the other children's coats or books when they were dropped, and never grew angry when he missed the soccer ball or couldn't add a column of numbers, many children liked Harvey and became his friends.

He grew stronger and healthier each year, and slowly his sunken cheeks began to fill out. He continued to live with his new family but also kept some contact with those who remained in his Blackfoot family. He learned that one of his own family members had hung himself and another had just had a baby at age fourteen. Despite these tragedies, he respected his native family and all the traditions, but he knew he was getting medical care, an education, and advantages he wouldn't have had without the Thompsons. However, the most important thing to him was that he had learned about the Church from them.

He said "Thank you" often to his new family and began calling Susan and Richard "Mom" and "Dad." Harvey told his new mom what he wanted most of all: "I want to be able to stay with you and become a member of the Church."

So his new parents obtained permission from the Children's Guardian for the Province of Alberta and the Blackfoot Tribe for Harvey to be baptized. After the baptism, Harvey hugged his family and finally felt as though he had sent down roots and belonged there.

As a teenager he watched his older sisters water-ski while he tossed the rope out the back of the boat. He pulled in their skis when they finished, but because he couldn't imagine himself sliding across the water on wooden slabs, he shook his head when his folks asked him if he'd like to ski. Susan almost had to force him out of the boat, but after a few tries, Harvey stood up on water skis. He grinned broadly, and tears from his own eyes blended with the spray from his skis. Here was something he could do well.

He was only five feet three at age fifteen when he began attending a vocational high school that offered a special program for children with learning disabilities. Harvey developed into an honor student in that program.

Harvey also loved the Scouting program. He was always one of the first to finish canoe trips and hikes and insisted on making the campfires, sometimes with only a few twigs to start the flame. One day he told his parents he wanted to try for Canada's highest Scouting achievement, the Queen's Venturer Award. He knew it would offer many challenges and would be very difficult for him, but he was determined to do it. He wanted to prove that he was a regular kid and that sickness and learning disabilities should not keep a person from succeeding. All anyone needed to do was to work hard and trust in God.

Harvey worked hard for three years. He visited nursing homes, carted heavy gear to many campsites, and learned to tie all kinds of knots in ropes. He built fences not too far from the Church for his service project.

At age seventeen one obstacle stood between him and his reception of the Venturer Award. He had to pass the first-aid course, which required him to write an exam. Harvey knew he couldn't pass the written part. The Scout leader did not realize Harvey had a learning disability because he spoke easily with people, cooperated, and followed directions so well, but when the instructor learned of Harvey's special circumstances, she allowed him to take an oral exam instead.

Harvey told his parents afterward, "It took me years to do this, and the test was hard. I was scared and didn't want to forget anything. That was one of the hardest things I have ever done."

At the award ceremony for Scout Canada, held in the Calgary Jubilee Auditorium, the Queen's Scout Awards would be given to those who had achieved their Venturer status. Scouting officials asked Harvey, then eighteen, if he would give the reply in behalf of all the Scouts. Harvey, in his usual accepting nature, replied, "Oh, sure."

Harvey saw his dad break out in a cold sweat when he accepted the assignment, but Harvey knew he could do it. God would make his mind clear and help him to think. His dad worked with him on a speech for several hours, and he sensed his father's concern that he wouldn't be able to remember this five-minute speech, but Harvey wasn't worried. Both he and his dad prayed silently for help.

Just before the Scouting ceremony, with fifteen hundred

people in attendance, Harvey heard his dad explain to
the Scouting officials that Harvey might have some difficulties delivering his speech and that they should be prepared to help him if he got stuck. Harvey saw his dad's
knitted brows and watched his mom squeezing her hands
together. He thought, "They really love me." Harvey felt
exhilarated and wasn't too worried, because he had done
hard things before. Facing people who thought he was
strange was harder, but a friendy smile was all it usually
took to encourage them.

He stood behind the podium, beaming, while he spoke
in a clear, steady tone, delivering his speech with ease,
although inside, his heart raced as he stared at the huge
crowd. Then emotion cracked his voice. "I am proud to be
in the Venturer program. It produces winners, and we
are *all* winners."

The members of the audience pulled out tissues, applauded, and cheered in a standing ovation for two full
minutes when Harvey finished and handed flowers to
Judge Skibo.

Newspapers reported that Harvey Calfrobe, a young
native, a foster child who once had been told he wouldn't
live and who had struggled with learning disabilities,
received the Queen's Venturer Award, one of only six
recipients in the nation and possibly the only native in
Canada to ever receive this highest achievement.

As a priest in the Calgary Eighth Ward, Harvey continued to demonstrate courage. He told his parents, "I
believe in the Church. It really inspires me a lot and helps
me to help others. I believe God lives, and I want to go on
a mission."

Combined choir in Lauluväljak,
Estonia, singing nationalistic songs

Jaanus Silla

OPENING THE CHURCH IN ESTONIA

PARENTS
Kolja and Mai Silla

LOCATION OF STORY
Estonia

Jaanus fumbled to open the letter, his fingers icy cold. He read the return address and knew what the letter would say. He was in his last year in high school in Harjumaa, Estonia, and he knew that the letter would announce his time to fill out his papers to serve in the Red Army. He sensed something missing in his life, but he didn't think it was the army.

His mother placed a bowl of meat and pea soup before him and sliced some rye bread. "Eat your supper, Jaanus. You need your strength."

"I don't want to go into the army," he told her, "because I have heard too many bad things." He handed her the letter.

Jaanus watched drops of perspiration form above her lip as she read the letter. She placed the letter on the table and turned her head. "I know," she said, "but everyone must serve."

Jaanus continued, "It's what I have heard from other

177

boys who have come back to their families. The seniors—
they persecute the juniors. It is tradition."

His mother pulled grey strands of hair behind her
ears, but she said nothing.

"It's worse than you know," he said. "The seniors abuse
the juniors mentally and sexually."

His mother covered her face and nodded her head.
"We must think of something."

"I have heard that even in the United States many
young people have demonstrated and refused to serve in
that army," Jaanus explained.

"I have spoken very little to you of politics as a youth,"
his mother answered, "because I have not wanted to do
anything wrong."

Jaanus reassured her, "I understand, Mother. Many
people have been afraid that if their children slipped and
said something against the Communist regime, the parents would be watched and maybe sent to prison. So about
some issues, everyone is quiet."

Jaanus leaned against the window and looked out. He
had always been aware of an undercurrent of political
whispering and hushes from lips too frightened to speak
openly, even in small city apartments such as their own.
This contrasted sharply with the raucous noise of the city
that Jaanus could hear outside his window: grinding
gears of cotton textile mills, the honking of cars and buses,
the clang of trolleys, children yelling, and parents shouting as they bargained over veal and dairy products. His
problem still perplexed him when he fell asleep that
night.

In the morning, he spoke some more with his mother.
He whispered to her as they ate rye bread and jam. "We
watch Finnish TV and learn that things might be better
in some other places, but I have not read much literature
about the rest of the world. The government tries to show

we are the best, such as saying the Soviet Union produces more metals than anyone else."

"Shhh," his mother blew between her teeth. "Most countries teach that their way is the best, I think."

"Our school history books tell us that the Communist government is trying to prevent wars, that we are peaceful. Maybe it is true, and maybe it is not true."

"We should not talk like this." His mother wrung her hands.

"Mother, I see boys come home from the army like they are dead." He stuffed a hunk of dark bread in his mouth. "Army life would change my life forever, and I would have to give up photography."

In the middle of the night, Jaanus suddenly awoke and then lay in bed with his hands cupped behind his head. He stared up at a bare lightbulb hanging from the ceiling. When he tried to imagine what army camp life might be like, he shuddered.

He remembered how simple life used to be when he was younger. He recalled running through birch and aspen groves with his mother, fishing for pike in the Keila River with friends. Although his parents had divorced when he was only two, his mother had always provided for him, working as an agriculturalist. They had lived in many small cities in Estonia, usually in two-room apartments. He didn't want to leave this peaceful life for the army.

The more he thought, the lower he sank into his bed. His mother had told him a few things about God when he was younger. Sometimes they had attended a Christian church at Christmas after trimming their tree with candles and waiting for Jôuluvana, the Estonian Santa Klaus.

A warmth crept into his chest. He had not really prayed before. "Help me, please, to find a way to avoid this army life," he thought. "Father in Heaven, if you *are,* then help me."

When he appeared at his physical examination with the doctor, he hoped the man would find something wrong with him. In fact, Jaanus imagined many possible health problems that he reported to the doctor, because he knew others had also done this. The doctor appeared to know that his health problems were not serious, but he did find physical reasons why Jaanus was not fit to serve. Other officials signed his army passport indicating that he never needed to serve. Jaanus thanked God, breathed more easily, and stopped awakening abruptly in the night.

When he finished high school, he did not enter the army. Instead he worked in a photo studio, developing film and studying photography for a year. He loved the odor of developing fluid, and many mornings he awoke early to snap pictures of people walking along Pärnu Maantee. Or some weekends, he rode the train to a marshy area and took photos of the sunset. Several of his photos were printed in the *Teater Muusika Kino,* a music-cinema magazine.

While he snapped pictures, his mother grew more interested in spiritual things, bringing home written accounts of people who reported out-of-body experiences. It piqued the interest of Jaanus too, who was always hungry for truth.

He went to Saaremaa, an island, to meet a spiritualist personally. Although Jaanus asked him many questions about God, the man had no answers that satisfied him. When Jaanus realized the spiritualist wanted some money from him, Jaanus received a bad feeling and left. This was not the knowledge that he was seeking.

At the same time that Jaanus began searching for spiritual truth, tremors of political change had begun to softly shake the leaves of Estonian life. Jaanus watched with interest as clusters of students gathered at a rock festival in Tartu, Estonia, and brazenly waved a dozen blue, black, and white flags, the Estonian flag from before Communist occupation.

Communist television reporters who covered the incident edited out all the footage that showed students with independence flags. "Why do they do this?" Jaanus wondered.

Students complained to occupation leaders: "It is not right that you should edit out the most important part of the coverage." Shortly after, independence flags popped up like dandelions.

People began to question the government openly for the first time. At the folk festival in Latvia, Estonians raised their flag. Latvians and Lithuanians copied the example and pulled out their own frayed flags, while students made up patriotic songs. Two years later, thirty-eight thousand people would join in one combined choir in Lauluväljak, Estonia, to sing nationalistic music, while five hundred thousand citizens would travel to listen to the performance.

Jaanus shared his thoughts with his mother. "People are wondering why the government is not more interested in our culture. People are calling this the 'Singing Revolution' because Estonians are singing patriotic songs instead of fighting."

Jaanus participated in these activities along with his friends. One evening they carried the Estonian flag, fluttering over their shoulders, on the way to a patriotic song party in Lauluväljak. Enraged police saw the flag and chased them down the Pärnu Maantee. When they caught them, the police grabbed the flag and ripped it, but Jaanus and his friends were only reprimanded, and their pride flamed higher.

"There is a special feeling in Estonia," Jaanus later

explained in an excited voice to his mother. "People are patriotic. We all feel this new warmth and happiness."

His mother's eyes darted over her shoulder, but she appeared to be growing used to Jaanus's open talk.

Despite protest from Communist officials, a declaration was written on February 22, 1990, urging the Supreme Soviet to begin negotiations for independence. Jaanus cheered when free elections were permitted in March to elect a rival parliament. By May 8, 1990, the Supreme Council restored the Republic of Estonia, with its patriotic flag and emblem.

During the burst of patriotism, Jaanus also searched for spiritual truth and began to investigate the Baptist religion. The Baptists treated him with friendliness and invited him to their homes, and at first the religion appeared to be what he had felt lacking in his life, and he scheduled his baptism in their church. However, he still harbored questions in his mind: Why are there not any more apostles? What is the purpose of this life?

Then a few days before Christmas, when Jaanus was to be baptized, he was in the Baptist chapel with three friends. Feeling the spirit of Christmas, Jaanus wanted to help people in some way, but when he and his friends discussed it, they didn't know how.

Enn Lembit, a thirty-year-old, bearded man, who was there talking to other church members, spoke also to Jaanus and his friends. He stated, "I have a new testimony about Christ and what prophets say nowadays. Come to my house to hear about this wonderful news."

"Imagine that," Jaanus thought, "a prophet speaking to people on earth today!" His spine tingled as he and his friends went to Enn Lembit's apartment for a meeting in November 1989.

At that first meeting, Enn Lembit explained, "My father-in-law, Valtteri Rötsä, was converted to the Mormon Church in Finland. He returned to Estonia to his family with his pockets full of literature about the Mormon faith." Enn's eyes shone with enthusiasm as he explained the gospel message to Jaanus and others in that small room.

"This is simple and easy to understand," Jaanus spoke to his friend Urmas Raavik.

About an hour after the meeting had started, Brother Uusituba, a businessman from Finland, read the challenge in Moroni 10:3–5. He suggested that they pray and ask God if this Church were true.

Jaanus thought, "I feel really good in this home, and I like what he is saying." When they prayed, he felt a warm glow and believed that the gospel was true. He said to a friend, "I am happy that God's plan seems so perfect."

Following the meeting, Jaanus rushed home with a flushed face and sat his mother down on the worn couch. "I have found something wonderful," he said. "I just attended the first meeting of the true church in Estonia, and I am happy that I had the faith to find it. I know you believe in Jesus Christ, and I want you to come with me." Jaanus took his mother to the first sacrament meeting held in Estonia.

On December 16, 1989, Enn Lembit was baptized as the first member to join The Church of Jesus Christ of Latter-day Saints in Estonia. On December 17, 1989, Jaanus hopped off the bus at Laagri on the outskirts of Tallinn and hunted for a different church meeting place in the Viru Hotel, which had a pool that could be used for baptisms. As the wind blew dry snow past fourteenth-century houses and into his face, he pulled his collar tightly around his neck. He grew frustrated because he couldn't find the right address, and finally gave up and returned home.

Later he learned that four people had been baptized that day in the hotel swimming pool, and Jaanus felt even more frustrated. He had to wait anxiously for three more weeks until January 6, 1990, when he and his mother were baptized by Elder Aho in the Viru Hotel pool.

Jaanus and his friend Urmas Raavk decided that they must spread the gospel. They spoke with at least fifty people on the streets and knocked on twenty doors. They tried to talk like missionaries, explaining the story of Joseph Smith and the Book of Mormon. Jaanus explained to the contacts, "We have good friends in this city, the missionaries of the true gospel, and we would like you to come and meet them. They have information about a church that has twelve apostles and a prophet now like there was when Jesus organized his church." Many people came to meetings just to see the Americans.

The missionaries later asked Jaanus, "Why did you do that? Who gave you the authority to act as missionaries without asking us?"

"We knew from reading in the Bible that everybody must be a missionary," Jaanus answered. "I already have a strong desire to serve. It is hard to wait until I get a mission call."

The elders smiled and slapped Jaanus's shoulders. "In opening a new mission, we need to be very careful and only work through referrals to members' friends," they explained.

Jaanus would later learn that when President Steven R. Mecham of the Finland Helsinki East Mission first went into Estonia, the people turned on music or talked out in hallways with him. They wouldn't talk without creating background interference noise for fear of getting in trouble with the government. Slowly, President Mecham convinced them it was better to talk openly and to not hold any secrets from government officials.

President Mecham assumed that the Church was being monitored. He explained to Jaanus that Communist officials were very aware of the mission president's role in Estonia. One Communist official had told him, "You people really do what you say you do." The official had appeared to be both amazed and impressed, and President Mecham said that this openness proved to be important in getting the Church accepted. Proselyting needed to be handled carefully so as not to offend.

From then on, Jaanus and Urmas worked with the missionaries.

Estonia was dedicated by Elder Russell M. Nelson in the spring of 1990 in Laulalava in Estonia. On June 29 the Estonian government officially recognized the Church.

The laws of the land required that an Estonian church member who did not hold a position in the Estonian branch presidency be designated as president of the Church in Estonia. That person must sign the petition for the Church to become recognized there.

President Mecham asked Jaanus, "Would you consent to be the Church spokesperson to testify before the Minister of Religion and sign the petition as president?"

Jaanus was puzzled. "There are many people who could do that. I am only one."

"We would like you, Jaanus, to be the authorized person to sign the document because you have demonstrated such leadership."

Jaanus lowered his eyes. "I will do as you ask."

Jaanus testified before the Minister of Religion that The Church of Jesus Christ of Latter-day Saints was a legitimate church working in the country to help people and that the programs were not contrary to any laws of government.

Then Jaanus picked up the pen, remembering that he had been at the first meeting of the Church in Estonia, had attended the first official sacrament meeting, and was one of the first youth to be baptized. However, like many pioneers, he didn't yet fully comprehend how pivotal his action was when he signed his name on the president's line. Twenty others signed their names below his signature.

Jaanus thought about the sequence of events in his life over the past two years and considered how different things might have been if he had entered the army. Instead, he had found spiritual truth.

After signing, Jaanus told President Mecham, "This is a great country to have such things happen here, but we have had difficult times too. Many people have open hearts, and they will easily accept the truth of God. The Church will grow fast, and I am only one small piece."

President Mecham said, "Yes, that's true, but you were chosen, Jaanus, because we felt you were a kind of team leader, the first of eight young men given the Melchizedek Priesthood in Estonia. You have been a wonderful example, very diligent, quiet, and effective. You have been sincere in bearing your testimony, providing a sweet spirit of reassurance and a beacon of light and hope to other young people."

POSTSCRIPT: Jaanus was called to the Utah Salt Lake City Mission on January 16, 1991.

64th ANNUAL
SCRIPPS HOWARD
NATIONAL SPELLING BEE
1991

Velma Kee at the national spelling bee

Velma as a young girl

Velma Kee in native dress

BE ALL YOU CAN BEE

PARENTS
Larry and Lavern Kee

LOCATION OF STORY
Window Rock, Arizona

Thirteen-year-old Velma Kee wiped her damp hands on the sides of her cotton skirt. In just a few minutes the Arizona State spelling bee would begin, and that day, April 7, was her last chance to win the state title because next year she would be too old to compete again.

She clasped her squash-blossom necklace as she glanced around the ornate room at the twenty-four other participants in the Hyatt Regency in Phoenix. At five feet one and only ninety-five pounds, she felt quite small. Only one other Native American was participating, and she wondered if the judges were surprised to see two representatives from the reservation.

She watched as two boys laughed and jabbed each other with their elbows, while some contestants sat on edges of their chairs clasping the sides with stiff arms. Velma forced herself to relax, because she had a little over half an hour to think, to remember. News reporters had asked her many times what had motivated her to become a "human spell-check." Where had her interest originated?

Her mother had told her that she had begun learning words when she was a baby on the Navajo reservation in Tonalea, Arizona. When she was ten months old, her father had propped her on top of the dresser that divided the one-room house in half.

"Listen to my child," her father spoke to her maternal grandmother. "Velma, say . . . 'ba . . . by.'"

Velma grinned with the attention. "Ba . . . by," she repeated.

"Say . . . 'el . . . e . . . phant,'" her mother chimed in.

"El . . . phant," Velma repeated.

Her grandmother peered into her face. "Spa . . . ghet . . . ti."

"Pa . . . ghet . . . ti," Velma copied without pausing.

Her mother whisked her into her arms. "You are very tiny, but you must have a big brain."

"Maybe she's not that smart," her grandmother said, laughing, as Velma stuffed a handful of her mother's black hair into her mouth and chewed.

When she was three, Velma had clung to her mother's skirt as her mother prepared to leave for work. "I want to learn to count to one hundred," Velma begged.

"I have to leave now, Velma. We can do it later when we drive to the trading post to get water."

"I want to learn it now."

"Okay, I'll write them for you."

Velma sat on the bed near the butane stove and read the numbers to herself all day. Her grandmother could hardly make her stop to eat a plate of potatoes for lunch. With no electricity, Velma could see best in the light of the blazing sun, so she didn't want to eat until dark.

When she heard the rumble of her mother's truck in the evening, she jumped off the bed, threw the door open, and exclaimed, "Mommy, Mommy, listen. I know them all—all the way to one hundred." Velma held the paper in front of her like a trophy as she leaned against the government-built house. Patches of chicken wire showed through the flaking cement wall.

In just a few days she also learned the vowels, the consonants, and their sounds. As her mother read mail-order books to her, Velma repeated them back in the exact words. By the time she entered preschool, she could read several children's books, a handful of wrinkled Archie comic books, and the cartoons saved from bubble-gum wrappers, which she stashed under her bed. Her teacher tested her skills in kindergarten and discovered Velma could read on a second-grade level.

Her parents moved several times as they found employment in Red Lake, Tuba City, Page, Ganado, and Fort Defiance on the reservation. Several brothers joined the family, most of them thin and on the small side, like her parents: Timothy, a year younger; Randy, who loved animals and kept a rabbit hutch under the front steps at Fort Defiance; Monty, the only chubby member of her family; and Donnie; but there were no sisters for Velma, and *that* was hard for her.

Her paternal grandmother shared her house with them in Ganado when Velma was in elementary school. Her father laid tracks on the Southern Pacific Railroad, and her mother worked thirty miles away in Window Rock at the food-stamp office.

Velma and her family slept in a round hogan with a dirt floor outside her grandmother's house. In the winter they built a fire in the center to keep warm. Although they still had to haul water, her grandmother had electricity, and Velma discovered television, learning many new words as commercials flashed across the screen.

Her fourth-grade teacher entered Velma in her first

spelling bee, and with Velma's quick memory, she won fourth place in the school. She took her certificate home and hid it under her bed so her brothers couldn't destroy it.

One spring day when Velma was in fifth grade and living at Fort Defiance in a trailer with her parents and brothers, she sat outside chewing on a fat piece of fry bread. She watched Timmy, Randy, and Monty tearing around, shooting each other with homemade stick guns. She watched them dig huge holes in the yard, large enough to hide inside.

She didn't want to play their games. The hot sun burned the top of her head and sucked the moisture from the ground. Sagebrush stretched for miles in every direction, one of the few plants hardy enough to grow in the parched land. Words were easy for Velma, but to be so alone was really hard. If only she had a sister to play with . . .

"Guess what?" her mother came outside and said. "I'm going to have another baby."

Velma asked hopefully, "Do you think it will be a girl?"

"We'll just have to wait and see."

Velma ran into her bedroom in the trailer, closed the door, reached for her spiral-notebook journal that she kept under her bed, and began to write. "Maybe I'll finally get a sister," she said aloud.

Although her father still leaned toward Navajo beliefs, Velma followed the example of her mother, who had been an Indian placement student, and her grandmother, who was also a Mormon, even though her family hadn't attended church for years. She kneeled down on the carpet and prayed, "Please let me have a sister. Please make the baby be a girl."

Months later, when Dorianne was born, Velma bubbled with excitement, but she didn't show her emotions, which she usually kept locked inside. Her prayers had been answered, and she finally had a baby sister.

"See your baby sister, Velma," her mother said when she returned from the hospital in Fort Defiance.

"Look, Mom, her hair is like black dandelion fluff," Velma said as she laughed. "Look, she's squeezing my finger." Here was her friend, her companion, and mentally she spelled it: "C-o-m-p-a-n-i-o-n." Velma helped change Dorianne's diapers and held her in her lap when she cried.

Within the week, however, baby Dorianne developed a cold, then a rash that would not clear up. Velma watched the red spots on her baby sister's face spread until her whole face was one crimson blotch.

Velma hovered over Dorianne's fretful sleep. "Get better, Dorianne," she whispered.

Dorianne cried, squealed, and writhed until Velma's mother took her back to a doctor in Fort Defiance.

"What's wrong with her?" Velma asked when her mother returned after several trips to the doctor.

Her mother's hair, which was usually fluffed in layers about her head, hung in damp strings. "She has a low white-blood cell count."

"What does that mean?" Velma asked.

"It means she can't fight off germs."

"Will she get better?" Velma's throat tightened.

Her mother sat down at the kitchen chair and rested her head in her hands. "It means she has what is called SCIDS."

"What's that?"

"It stands for Severe Combined Immune Deficiency Sickness."

Velma spelled the words in her mind. It was a long title and sounded bad. "But will she get better?"

"I have to take her to specialists in San Francisco. The doctor thinks they can treat her better there."

Dorianne started to wail, and even though Velma tried to rock her in her arms, Dorianne squirmed, refusing to be comforted.

Velma clung to Dorianne as her mother prepared to leave for San Francisco. She kissed the tiny nose, the balled fists, and a tear fell onto Dorianne's red face. Dorianne looked up at her with large black eyes, partly swollen shut with puffy lids.

"I have to take her now, Velma." Her mother picked up Dorianne and whisked her out the door. They were gone that fast. She knew her father too would be leaving soon to work on the railroad for an entire month, and the loneliness already began closing around her like suffocating smoke. Velma stood for a long time at the door under an unusually grey sky and listened to the wind whistling through cacti and tumbling weeds.

Each day Velma dragged home from school and watched her younger brothers until her aunt or uncle arrived to help. She began memorizing spelling words by herself from her *Scripps Howard Spelling Bee Book*. She missed her mother, who used to listen to her while stirring up fry bread as Velma dictated words to her for an hour every night.

Her mother returned home with Dorianne a couple of times but could hardly pay attention to Velma. Velma talked to Dorianne and tried to sing and spell words to her, but each time Dorianne's sickness flamed hot, her mother snatched the baby into her arms and immediately returned to the specialist in San Francisco.

In the sixth grade Velma won first place in the Navajo Nation Bee and only third place in the state competition (because she accidentally repeated a consonant).

Even as she buried her face in the spelling book, her stomach burned with acid from a nervous worry for her sister. She kept pushing the feeling behind the words:

"convalescent, recuperate, robustious, siege, reign," she spelled. If she could just keep the "ei" and "ie" straight, everything would be okay.

Velma prayed into her pillow at nights. "Why are you making this happen? Please, God, make my sister better. I love her."

As Velma sat down to dinner with Uncle Alex one evening, she looked at his downcast face and sensed something was wrong. Then he shared the tragic words, words she had been hoping she would never hear: "Your baby sister has . . . died."

"No, she didn't," Velma argued. "She can't. Mother just took her back for more medicine."

When her father finally arrived, he called the children into the bedroom and gathered the boys in his arms. "The doctors could do nothing more. It is true. Dorianne has gone to the Great Spirit."

Salty tears stung Velma's cheeks, but she wanted to be strong for her brothers. She returned to the dinner table and bit off a few bites of a tortilla, blinking her eyes rapidly. After a few mouthfuls, she went to the bedroom and shut the door.

Velma pushed her face into the pillow to smother the sobs. "It's my fault. I know it is. If I hadn't prayed for a sister, this wouldn't have happened. God is punishing me." Her eyes searched her room for images of coyotes, owls, or pitch-black Navajo forms coming to taunt her, but she saw nothing. She cried into the middle of the night until her shaking rocked her to sleep.

The bishop who spoke at the funeral stated that Dorianne would live again, that she was a special spirit, but it didn't comfort Velma. Afterward, Velma walked around the trailer quietly to keep out of the way. She tried to ask her mother and her aunt questions, but no one seemed to want to talk about . . . death.

She knew that the traditional Navajo did not speak about the dead and feared the *chindi,* the evil ones, and the ghosts of departed spirits. Some of the older people even carried a pouch of gall medicine about their necks to ward off poison from corpses. However, her family was not traditional in that way. That couldn't be the reason for the silence, but not even her father wanted to talk about Dorianne's departed spirit. So she kept the questions inside and walked about with a long face, hoping that someone would notice her confusion, but no one did.

Each night she recorded her thoughts in the spiral-notebook journal and then cried herself to sleep. "It is my fault, and I must be punished," she wrote. "Maybe I should take my own life and go to sleep forever. Then the punishment would be finished." The thought of it brought some strange peace to her.

"Wake up, Velma. We're going to go to church," her mother's voice pierced through her sleep.

"I don't want to go." Velma covered her head with the blanket.

"Yes, you do. You and your brothers are coming with me."

It was the first time since she was tiny that her mother had suggested going back to church.

A few hours later, Velma found herself in the Merrie Miss class, sitting on a folding chair and staring at her teacher's wire-rimmed bifocals. "What if a person did something so bad that they had to kill themselves?" Velma asked.

Her teacher's eyes grew larger, and she was silent for a moment. "That is suicide, and that would be the next greatest sin to murder."

Velma's cheeks tingled with a strange fear.

"Sometimes things happen to us that we don't under-

stand," her teacher continued. "Sometimes we blame ourselves for things we didn't really do. These problems are
not God's fault, but they can make us stronger. Remember
that carbon changes into diamonds only under pressure."

That afternoon, Velma walked alone into the desert
and kicked her toe at a patch of rabbit brush, which bent
and then popped back. She watched a lizard scurry across
the hot dirt, leaving a tiny, wiggly trail behind. These
were her only friends—bushes, lizards, and butterflies.

She blinked her eyes and inhaled. Maybe it wasn't
her fault at all. Maybe Dorianne's death had just happened to make them all stronger, like her Merrie Miss
teacher had said. This time when she cried into her pillow
at night, it was a cleansing cry, draining away the poison
from her spirit.

Velma felt lighter the next day as she skipped down
the road to the school bus. Each time the old fear popped
into her head, she pushed it away. "It is not my fault,"
she repeated between clenched teeth. "I'm innocent—
I-n-n-o-c-e-n-t," she spelled. "Or was it 'ant'?" She had
always been stumped by "ent" or "ant." "It's 'ent,' I think,"
and she congratulated herself and boarded the noisy bus.

Velma was baptized when she was twelve, and in the
summer she attended the Young Women's camp in
Ramah, New Mexico, where she bore her testimony
around the campfire before the twenty-five girls present
and shared her experience about losing Dorianne. "I know
that maybe Dorianne was sent down here because Father
in Heaven had wanted us to be in the Church. My family
has pulled together more, and now my brothers, mother,
and I are attending church again. I know the Church is
true," she confided in a shaky, soft voice.

Spelling bee time rolled near again. Besides playing

the trumpet in the school band—until braces got in the
way—she maintained her status as an honor student,
enjoyed speech and drama, and still devoted several hours
a day to memorizing correct spellings. She won first place
in the Navajo Nation Bee again in seventh grade, but she
could never compete in nationals unless she won in the
state championship because the Navajo nation did not
even qualify for competition within the nation. She didn't
understand why not.

She practiced spelling an hour each day at school, and
sometimes she practiced several hours a day at home too.
The pages in her *Scripps Howard Spelling Bee Book*
developed wrinkles and smudges, and sometimes she felt
sick from worrying.

As the time approached for her eighth-grade bee and
her last chance to compete, her father spoke up. "I need to
take you to a medicine man to bless you before this bee."
He was only a few inches taller than she was, but his
voice was strong and sure, and she always listened to it.
"Every time you get to the last stage, something happens,
and you lose out on the last word. Maybe someone is
thinking evil thoughts of you, trying to hex you so that
you stumble and repeat a letter."

Velma didn't want to go and looked in confusion at
her mother. Her mother only nodded in her husband's
direction. Her unspoken words said, "Respect him. Do as
he says."

So Velma went to a medicine man, who surprised her
by wearing normal clothes. He built a fire, then pulled
out his medicine fire sticks, and sprinkled some herbs
and something powdery in the fire so it would smoke. He
picked up a feather and patted the smoke on her, at the
same time chanting a prayer to the Great Spirit, asking
for protection and for a good performance at the bee.

Velma felt strange, because she had participated in

something like this only once before when she was a baby, and she didn't remember it at all. The medicine man's prayer was sincere, but she still felt uncomfortable.

Just before the competition, her mother beckoned to her. "I have made an appointment with Bishop Brown to give you a priesthood blessing. Come with me. Your father did it the traditional way. Now I will take you to someone who has the power of God."

There was no fire, no smoke, no herbs or feathers, but when Bishop Brown rested his hands on her head, she felt a quiet peace enter her heart. It was small and not dramatic, but she felt her spirit lift as he told her that she would not be afraid, that she would be able to remember and speak clearly. Each night following the blessing, when she prayed for Dorianne, she also prayed that she would perform well in the competition.

Because Velma knew she couldn't compete nationally if she tried only for the Navajo Nation Bee, she headed for the state competition. Why was she so driven, and why was this spelling bee so important to her? She wasn't sure.

"Number One."

Velma was jarred out of her memory and into the present as she heard the first number called, and she forced her mind back to the Hyatt Regency, at the state spelling bee. The competition had begun.

Suddenly she knew why she had devoted over thirteen hundred hours studying the correct spellings of words, and she wrote it down for a news reporter. "People on my reservation think Anglos win everything. I want them to know we're as good as anyone else. I am doing this for myself and my people."

They competed round after round, spelling such words as "trypanosome, osteogenesis, yannigan." Her mind performed as a tape recorder playing back correct spellings, and she didn't stumble or repeat letters.

Several hours later, two contestants remained: Alex Ong, an eighth grader from another school, and Velma.

It was Alex's turn. He stood up, tall and thin, his raised chin giving him a confident look.

"Pourboire," the moderator spoke in a loud, crisp voice.

Alex's face flushed. "Definition, please?" he asked.

Was he stalling for time, Velma wondered?

The moderator cleared her throat. "Pourboire—a tip or gratuity—pourboire."

Alex carefully spelled the word: "P-o-u-r-b-o-i-r."

Velma waited for the final "e," but Alex stopped after the "r." Velma felt heat race up her neck.

"Incorrect." The onlookers gasped as the moderator turned toward Velma. "If you spell this word correctly and one additional word, you have won the bee. If not, we return to Alex for another round."

Velma nodded her head in understanding. "Pourboire," she repeated to herself, her mind clear as the Arizona sky. "P-o-u-r-b-o-i-r-e," she spelled, smiling.

"Correct."

Again the audience gasped and whispered.

"The next word is 'oxylophyte.'" The moderator raised her eyebrows and stared at Velma.

Velma felt a moment's panic. "Definition, please?"

"Oxylophyte—a plant that prefers or is restricted to acidic soil."

Velma thought about Dorianne, about her blessing, about growing up on an acidic soil, and took a deep breath. "Oxylophyte. O-x-y-l-" She paused, then started again. "O-x-y-l-o-p-h-y-t-e."

"The spelling is correct." The moderator dabbed her forehead, and the crowd applauded. Velma was the first

Native American whom anyone could remember winning the state spelling bee.

She was handed a large bronze trophy with a cup on top. Reporters snapped her picture and asked her, "What made you want to do this?" This time she was prepared.

"The U.S. government provides welfare and food stamps, but we don't have to use them," she said, her voice quiet but strong. "There are many able people who get welfare and are satisfied. There are many bright minds wasted and destroyed by drugs and alcohol. These are things I don't understand." She paused to wipe her eyes and swallow. "We are humans lowering ourselves to animals. We should be humans rising to be gods."

POSTSCRIPT: From May 26 to June 1, Velma competed in the national spelling bee in Washington, D.C. She won fourth place.

Tam Nguyen as a young boy,
above; as a teenager, top;
and as a missionary, right

TAM NGUYEN

EDUCATION FIRST

PARENTS
Thanh and An T. Nguyen

LOCATION OF STORY
Saigon, Vietnam, and Tallahassee, Florida

Tam Nguyen was born in Saigon before the Communist takeover, and he lived there until he was four years old. He was the youngest child and the only boy in his family, and from the beginning his mother stressed the importance of getting a good education. "You must learn to read these words," she commanded as she read to him, "and then you can do great things."

Often his sister Linh, who was five years older than Tam, read to him too, and he respected her knowledge.

Since his father was in the army, his family sometimes lived on military bases, where the sounds of marching boots, shouting men, and exploding bombshells often frightened him. His sister Lan, who was one year older than Tam, sometimes became lost among the rows of identical green tents. The metal toilets were up on a hill, and he hated to use them because of the terrible odor. Most of the time he had only rice to eat, and in the evenings when darkness shrouded the camp, the only light came from the movie projector at the back of the camp.

Tam's mother worked for the American Embassy as a secretary. She later explained to Tam that just three weeks before the Communist takeover and the fall of Saigon on April 25, 1975, her boss told her that if she wanted to escape and ensure the safety of her children, she must pack one suitcase and bring her kids right away. She hurried home and packed the skimpiest essentials in one cloth bag, grabbed her three children, and left.

They scrambled aboard a noisy, green plane to join hot and damp refugees piled and tumbled together like clothes in an overloaded dryer. Tam's oldest sister, Linh, who was nine, carried her younger sister, Lan. His sisters' short black hair was trimmed straight as if a bowl had been put over each of their heads. Tam's mother carried the cloth bag and four-year-old Tam.

Not understanding what was happening, Tam anxiously clung to his mother in the camp in Guam where their papers were processed. They were flown to California and lived a year in a refugee camp near San Diego, where they slept in tents and stood in long lines each day for meals, as did hundreds of other refugees.

His mother managed to barter for everything they needed, including coats in an unusually cold spell. Tam brushed the overgrown shock of black hair from his eyes and looked at his strong mother adoringly.

"We must get your hair trimmed, Tam," his mother said, laughing. "Someone might think you are a wild panther."

Tam's mother constantly reminded him and his sisters, "Be strong. America is a land of opportunity—you can do anything you want to do. All you have to do is get a good education. You must always consider your education above everything."

"Yes, Mother," Tam and his sisters said and bowed their heads.

Doctor Washburne's family sponsored the Nguyens and introduced them to American customs, food, and The Church of Jesus Christ of Latter-day Saints. Tam's mother explained that she saw similarities between LDS beliefs and Vietnamese customs: the respect, the importance of family, and the emphasis on being industrious and getting a good education. When Tam's family joined the Church, Tam accepted the gospel the same way he accepted the American food placed in his hands, but he didn't understand it.

The Nguyens moved to Florida to be near friends, renting a little wooden shack in Tallahassee in a poor neighborhood where the grass grew tall enough around the house for Tam to hide in. He'd wake up in his bed at night and try to smash reddish roaches scurrying on his bedroom wall. Thefts occurred regularly, and street fights exploded in the heated evenings.

Tam's father had not lived with them since Saigon, and finally his mother got an official divorce. She then worked two, sometimes three, jobs trying to improve their conditions. Over the next few years, Tam and his family moved through several apartments in an effort to find a good neighborhood. As Tam grew taller, he watched his mother wear his and his sisters' old clothes so that she wouldn't have to buy anything for herself.

She constantly said to Tam, "You three will get a good education. You will become important people. We will help each other to do that."

They supported each other and stuck together. When Tam was in third grade, some older bullies threatened to beat him because he was an Asian. "We will grab you after school and smash your face," they boasted.

Although Tam hurried out after school to escape them, the bullies caught him.

As they began to shove him around, Linh jumped in

front of him, her small body a shield. "Don't you dare touch him! He's my brother." She threw her hands on her hips.

Tam looked at his sister's defiant stance and puffed out his chest. He saw the surprise in the older boys' eyes. They elbowed each other, shouted insults, and then left.

"Wow, Linh," Tam said. "You were really neat. If you ever need help, I'll save you too."

Linh smiled and squeezed his hand as they scampered home together.

The bishop of their ward asked Tam's mother to be his secretary. Tam enjoyed the ward where they lived, especially playing basketball in the church gym. On one Thanksgiving day when his mother could afford only a chicken, the members brought them a turkey along with a basket of food.

When his mother finally saved enough money, they moved into a subdivision six miles out of Tallahassee. His family stopped going to church, because his mom had to work on Sundays.

When Tam was in high school, his home teacher, Jack Nelson, asked, "Why don't you and Lan come to seminary? Someone can come by to pick you up in the mornings."

"What time?" Tam asked.

Brother Nelson smiled. "Brace yourselves. It starts at 5:30."

"Five-thirty! Are you serious?"

In spite of the early hour, Tam and Lan attended seminary for a few weeks, but although the students were friendly, Tam didn't understand the gospel discussions. Thinking he didn't belong, he quit attending.

Tam played football and was captain of the soccer team in high school. In his spare time, he worked at the daily newspaper, taking complaint calls. He gave part of his money to his mother to help pay the utility bills. When Linh needed help with tuition at the University of Florida, he sent her several hundred dollars at a time. He also managed to buy a used Toyota so that he could chug around town. He would never forget his mother's words, "Education must come first," so at the same time, he maintained straight A's at school.

Most of Tam's friends were the athletes on the school teams until he developed a friendship with Marika, a classmate and a Latter-day Saint.

"You're different from other girls," Tam told her one day. "You can talk about issues and discuss serious things." He was pleased when they were placed in four classes together. Mustering his courage, Tam asked Marika for a date, and she accepted.

They went to a movie and a fast-food place, and Tam had a great time with her. The next day in humanities class, however, when Marika left the class briefly, Tam had a strong urge to read her journal, which she had left on her desk, to see what she had thought about their date. He was shocked to read, "He didn't hold any doors open for me or do anything polite like that. He wasn't at all what I had expected . . . " Tam felt as if he had just been slapped in the face.

When Marika returned, she asked, "What's wrong, Tam? You look so sad." She adjusted the headband in her long hair and pulled a face, probably to make him laugh.

"Oh, nothing." Tam smiled weakly.

"There is something wrong. I can tell."

After everyone had left the class, Tam and Marika stayed behind even though the teacher turned the light off, and they were left in the darkened room. "Now tell me what's wrong," Marika repeated.

After much coaxing, Tam confessed, "I couldn't resist it. I read your journal to see what you thought of our date.

I'm really sorry. I don't usually do that." He looked down. "But if you can forgive me, will you give me another chance?" He expected her to be mad at him for reading the journal. Instead they talked, and she agreed to give him another chance.

He began opening doors for her in an exaggerated way every time he saw her, in the hall, in the classroom, everywhere they went. Finally she laughed and said, "It's okay, Tam."

One evening he sat on Marika's porch with her. She began telling him the Joseph Smith story. As he listened to the crickets chirping and Marika's soft voice, he wondered what Joseph might have been thinking when the Father and the Son appeared to him, a mere boy, and when he received the plates. Tam felt the presence of the Holy Ghost.

"Tam," Marika said. "Why don't you start coming to seminary?"

Tam agreed. This time as he began to read the Book of Mormon, it all began to make sense to him. He thought the book was so interesting that he read it every chance he got and finished it in six weeks, gaining a testimony of its truthfulness.

As a result, he lost interest in running around with his wild friends. Tam felt different and wanted very much to be better friends with the seminary students but he didn't know how to do it. He spent much of his senior year feeling lonely. But even when Marika got another boyfriend, he continued attending seminary regularly.

At the end of his senior year, Tam graduated as Salutatorian with the second highest grade point average in his class, and he delivered one of the speeches at the commencement ceremony.

Both of his sisters were already studying to be engineers, and Tam received two academic scholarships to pay his way through Florida State University. He thought he would like to go to medical school after his undergraduate studies.

One Sunday in priesthood meeting, Brother Nelson talked about missionary work and stated that he thought Tam would become a missionary someday. He gave him a missionary journal. Tam took the journal home, turned it over in his hands, and then placed it on the top shelf of his clothes closet and forgot about it.

Tam participated in all the youth activities and firesides that summer after his senior year. In the fall, after he began attending FSU, Hermann Buenning, his new home teacher and head of the Latter-day Saint Student Association, asked Tam, "How would you like to be one of twelve young people to start up the LDSSA?"

"I would like that very much," Tam answered. "What would I do?"

"Plan firesides and activities with the other youth leaders."

At last I can have a group of close Mormon friends, Tam thought. He knew how anxious his mother was for him to finish his education, but a kernel of desire had begun growing inside him to serve as a missionary. He started secretly setting aside money from his job at the FSU computer lab to help pay for a mission.

One evening Tam prayed, "Father, I may have a hard time getting on a mission, but I can be a missionary here. Please help me to find someone here who would want the gospel." He prayed for three weeks. At the computer lab, he shared his testimony with all his co-workers, everyone except Tichaona Matewa, whom his friends called "T." Since T was in a fraternity and enjoyed partying, Tam thought that he would be the last person who would be interested in the Church.

One afternoon Tam spoke to a friend at work. He told

him about Joseph Smith and the Book of Mormon. While
he was speaking, T walked into the room, sat down, and
listened. T's eyes widened in his black face, and then he
got up and left. Tam scratched his head and thought it
was strange. "Why would T listen?" he asked himself.

A couple of days later, Tam opened the door to walk
out of the office for the evening.

"Hey, Tam," a voice called from behind him.

Tam turned. He peered across the room. "T, is that
you? What are you doing in here?"

T was sitting alone in the darkened room. "Do you
think you could get me a copy of the Book of Mormon?" he
asked.

Tam's mouth dropped open. "You're joking? No, wait,
what am I saying? Well, sure—same as every good Mormon, I just happen to have one in the trunk of my car."

Tam took T to church with him, and his friend agreed
to listen to the missionaries. At the end of the first lesson,
the missionaries asked T if he wanted to be baptized, and
Tam was disappointed when T said he wasn't ready. He
prayed very hard that his friend would accept the Church.

Days later T entered the office and stopped at Tam's
desk. "I've been fasting and praying for three days," he
confided, his face tired and drawn.

Tam sucked in his breath.

"Do you think you could baptize me?" T grinned.

Tam leaped up from his chair and slapped his friend
on the back. "Wow! Baptize you? I'd love it."

It was his first experience baptizing anyone, and Tam
had difficulty controlling his emotions. He grew more
determined than ever to fulfill a real mission, and he
knew it was time to approach his mother.

He found her in the back yard on her knees in the
dirt, planting onions. He announced, "Mother, I'm going
on a mission."

She dropped her spade and shook the dirt from her small hands. "You don't tell your mother you're doing this. You don't tell her you're doing that. You ask for permission."

"Well, can you accept it?" he asked.

"No. The Church will still be around when you graduate. Education comes first. Then go on a mission."

"No, Mother," Tam insisted, "I need to go soon."

"I have no money to send you anyway. If you leave now, you will lose your scholarship and then come home to nothing. Why have I worked so hard to have you throw it all away?" She covered her face with dusty hands.

"Mother, I'll never forget all you have sacrificed for me, and I'll finish my education when I get back, but I have to go."

She squared her shoulders and stared him in the face. "That is not the Vietnamese way—a boy telling his mother."

Tam whispered in a soft voice. "I'm sorry, Mother, I don't want to hurt you, but this is not Vietnam." Then he kissed her cheek. "None of your effort will be thrown away, because I love you for all you have done, and I promise I'll finish my education."

Tam soon discovered that his mother had been right about his scholarship. He was told at the scholarship office that he would lose his financial support if he interrupted his education with a mission. Worse than that, he realized he did not have enough money saved to finance his mission, let alone his education.

He talked to his sister, Linh. She had graduated as a chemical engineer and had a good job. She said she remembered the many times Tam had sent her hundreds of dollars when she needed it for school. "I'll help to support you on your mission, Tam. We will always help each other."

For a moment Tam could see himself, a small, skinny third grader, with his sister standing defiantly in front of him, separating him from the bullies. He rubbed his sleeve over his eyes and hugged his sister.

Tam received a call to the San Antonio Spanish-speaking Mission, and his friend, T, was called as the first African-American to serve in the South African mission.

Tam packed his bag. He gave his furniture to a friend and his car to his mom. Just as he was to leave, he hurried back to his closet and pulled down the missionary journal given to him by Jack Nelson. He had come to America with one bag for his family. Now he stuffed his journal into one of three bags. "America, the land of opportunity," he whispered.

His mother stood at the bedroom door, blinking her eyes, but she held out her arms, and they hugged. "Be careful, Tam," she said. "And when you return home, be sure . . . "

"I know . . . be sure to finish my education. When I get home from my mission, Father in Heaven will help me find some way to complete college and become a doctor. I want to help other people, and I'll do that. Then I have another promise to keep for you, who've worked so hard for us." He kissed her forehead. "Then my sisters and I will give money to you, our mother, so that you can finally have your turn to get an education too."

Sebastian Van Dyke as
senior in high school ROTC

Sebi, #7; Ralph, #99

Rafael Van Dyke as senior
in high school band

Ralph, left, and Sebi, right, with mother

RAFAEL (RALPH) AND SEBASTIAN (SEBI) VAN DYKE
A DOUBLE TEAM

PARENTS
Frank and Mildred Van Dyke

LOCATION OF STORY
St. Augustine, Florida

As far back as Rafael Van Dyke could remember, he was hunting for the truth. When he was ten years old, he had sat on the carpet in his parents' bedroom with his twin brother, Sebastian, in their brick home in Spring Lake, North Carolina.

"How do you know God will take care of you?" Ralph rested his head on his mother's lap as she sat on the edge of her bed. He felt lonely, as if he were searching for something in a dream and couldn't find it.

"Son, I just know. 'You reap what you sow.' You just be the best you can be, and if you just be patient, God will bless you with everything you need."

Ralph looked up into his mother's deep, black eyes and knew he could always trust her, but why did he feel so lonely sometimes?

Later that night Ralph wandered through the living room on his way to bed and paused at the big family Bible lying on the carved stand. It was opened to the familiar passage his mother had underlined in Galatians 6:7, and he read, "For whatsoever a man soweth, that shall he also reap." It was one of her favorite scriptures, but for a moment it troubled him. What should he be reaping?

On the way to his bedroom, he thought about his brother, Sebi, who had been baptized in the Baptist church when he was eight, and wondered if that was what he was missing.

Sebi sat on the top bunk, on his fur blanket. His dad had brought them each a mink blanket when he was stationed in Korea in the army. He was holding a ruler in one hand and a wadded, paper ball in the other, and he smiled when he saw Ralph.

Sebi hit the paper ball with the ruler, and Ralph snatched it from the air, then yanked the ruler from Sebi. Sebi leaped from the top bunk and knocked Ralph to the floor. They wrestled and giggled until they dropped onto their bunks a half hour later.

Ralph lay on the bottom bunk, and he rubbed a hand over the soft fur. "Remember that day we were playing football, and Robbie got all mad and tried to beat me up?"

"Uh huh. We double-teamed him, and he backed off."

"And nobody's ever tried that on us again."

"And they never will as long as we stick together."

Ralph shoved the top bunk up with his foot. "Know what? I'm going to get baptized like you, Sebi."

Sebi leaned upside down over the top bunk and grinned. "Yeah, we're a team."

The next day, when Ralph told his parents of his decision, his mother hugged him.

His father said, "That's fine with me. Just stay away from the Mormon Church. They're devil worshipers."

So Ralph and Sebi attended the Baptist church together, sitting and listening with large, curious eyes. Ralph wanted to learn more about God so he could reap the right things, as his mother's Bible said. The members were friendly and kind to them and didn't seem to notice that they were the only two black members in the church.

The twin's first big encounter with racial prejudice didn't come from members in the Baptist church. It came from uncles, aunts, and cousins when everyone was gathered in the tidy brick house of Ralph and Sebi's grandmother. They looked sideways at boys, and one aunt said to their mother, "Just how come you let those boys fool around with those white folks? They should be going to the black church where they belong."

His mother, who had supported them in joining the church, replied, "Now you just leave my boys alone. They're good boys, and they have a right to go to any church they want to."

Ralph listened to the conversation in confusion, because he had thought his relatives would be proud of him and Sebi for trying to "reap" the truth about God.

As Ralph and his brother grew older, they grew more curious about doctrine. They quizzed their Baptist minister about what it meant to be saved and weren't satisfied with the answers they received.

"What if someone did something really terrible, like murder? Would he be saved too?" Sebi asked.

"Well," the teacher answered with kind, understanding eyes, "he'd still be saved, but it wouldn't be as good."

Always the peacemaker, Sebi didn't challenge the answer, but Ralph saw his knitted brows and guessed he wasn't satisfied.

"Why can't we dance?" Ralph interrupted. "What's wrong with dancing?" No matter what answer he heard, he could never imagine that dancing could be bad. Ralph still felt as if there were a missing puzzle piece, but for the moment, he shoved the thought aside.

By the time Ralph and Sebi began attending junior

high school, their legs had lengthened and their arms had grown gangly. Both he and Sebi wore nice shirts, knit ties, and dress shoes to school. They knew it wasn't a dress code, but about one-third of their school dressed this way. Ralph and Sebi watched some friends become involved with alcohol or drugs, but they stood side by side and said, "Why do you want to do that? It's bad for your health."

Other students liked and respected both boys for their beliefs. They always stood together on issues, and no one bothered them about their standards.

The boys devoted hours to basketball on their back-yard half court cemented in by their father, and they both made the junior high basketball team, which secured them more respect. Ralph also played the trombone and made first chair in seventh grade.

When Ralph and Sebi were fifteen, their parents announced that the family was moving to St. Augustine, Florida, where their dad would help run a service station with a brother. Many of Mr. Van Dyke's relatives lived in the area.

"You'll like St. Augustine," their father said. "It's the oldest city in the nation."

Their mother added with a chuckle, "I'm interested in finding that Fountain of Youth that's supposed to be there."

Ralph frowned at Sebi. Neither he nor Sebi wanted to move because they both had friends and were success-ful in academics and in sports, but they obediently packed their belongings, although they weren't happy about it.

They left behind their small brick house with red shutters, along with their basketball hoop in the back-yard. The yard at the new house had no room for a bas-ketball standard because it was small and had a cast-iron crab pot that was two feet high and chained to a pole. So his parents built fires beneath the huge pot and boiled crabs, while Ralph and Sebi went to the park near Orange Street to play ball.

On the first night in St. Augustine, Ralph met Steve Cybulski. Ralph and Sebi and five other guys were shooting layups when Sebi puffed, "What do you say we divide into teams?" His muscular arms shone with sweat.

"We're uneven," one of the five other boys said.

"Hey!" Ralph called to a guy playing alone on the other hoop. "You want to join us?"

The boy dribbled the ball toward them, his sandy hair damp with sweat. "Sure," he said. "Name's Steve," and he held out his hand.

After two heated games, Ralph and Steve dropped out and sat on the park bench to catch their breath.

"Where you from?" Steve wiped perspiration from his moustache and chin.

"We just moved from Spring Lake, North Carolina."

"You like the Tarheels?"

"That's been my team forever." Ralph rubbed his sweatshirt over his head. "You go to St. Augustine High?"

Sebi dropped down beside them.

"It's the only high school around here." Steve laughed. "You guys want me to pick you up?"

"It would sure beat catching the bus at six," Ralph answered.

"I just have an old yellow Opel. It's a plenty rusty old clunker, but it gets me around." Steve smiled.

Steve asked Ralph and Sebi at school, "You guys interested in playing church basketball? My dad's the coach."

"Sure," Ralph said, grinning. "We'd play basketball anywhere."

So Steve picked them up, and Ralph and Sebi played basketball at the Jacksonville Stake Center, and that's where they met the Mormon missionaries, who joined them in a game.

After the game, Elder Robert Wellman asked, "Would you guys like to listen to a gospel message? We're LDS missionaries, and we'd like to talk to you."

"Sure, I haven't got a problem with that," Ralph said, nodding his head. "How about you?" He looked at Sebi.

"If you want to, it sounds good to me."

Ralph felt a strange anticipation in his chest.

As they met at Steve's house, Ralph and Sebi asked again about being saved, but this time, as the missionaries put the puzzle together for them, including the part about eternal progression, it made sense to Ralph. All the pieces were there, and Ralph marveled because it was almost as though he had heard it before.

After a few sessions, the missionaries asked, "Are you two ready to be baptized?"

Ralph swallowed, and he looked at Sebi's lifted eyebrows. He could tell his brother wasn't sure yet, and they were a team. "We want to think about it," Ralph said. "We like what we're hearing, but we've already been baptized."

Elder Wellman explained, "But we have God's *authority*. That's different."

Supporting Ralph and also the missionaries, Sebi said, "We're not saying that we don't want to be baptized. We just want a little time to think about it."

After the next discussion on the restoration, Ralph felt a strong spirit. He knew these people were happier than others he knew, and he looked at Sebi hopefully. His brother nodded and smiled.

Ralph told his parents that they wanted to be baptized in the Mormon Church. His mother threw her arm around each of them, exclaiming, "I think that's a fine idea."

His dad frowned, and his moustache twitched. "I

warned you boys about that church, but if it's what you want, I won't try to stop you."

Ralph came out of the baptismal font, feeling complete, and he knew that this was what he had been searching for his entire life. He also realized with a jolt that this was why they had come to live in St. Augustine. His mother was so impressed at their baptism in January that she began the missionary lessons and joined the Church a month later.

At a family dinner, Ralph's grandmother threw her hands on her hips and complained, "I can't believe you all went and joined that white church." She shook the bandanna on her head. "You just think you're better than we are."

His mother disagreed. "We don't think we're better than anybody, but we ought to be able to go where we want and do what we want to do."

From then on, Ralph's relatives stopped calling, didn't invite them to their homes very often, and ignored them at family parties.

Both boys continued to play church ball and also made the high school basketball team, but a couple of black team members often smirked at them and jammed the ball in their faces. Ralph knew that they might think he and his brother were strange because of their beliefs, but he thought it was mostly because they made friends with white kids too. They were often looked at as traitors by black students. Ralph gave up the team first, and Sebi dropped off the team in his junior year.

They excelled in other ways. Sebi was chosen as cadet of the year in ROTC at the end of his sophomore year. Ralph was rewarded with first chair in the band.

Ralph didn't care what color people were. He just liked people, and his broad, friendly grin attracted others to him. He developed a friendship with a white girl in his

St. Augustine ward. They dated for a month, and then one day as he was on his way to English class, she shoved a note into his hands and hurried off down the hall.

Ralph felt a cold chill as he unfolded the paper and read, "My parents don't think we should date anymore because we are so different. I like you. I'm sorry, but I have to do what they say . . ."

He crumpled the note in his fist and chucked it in the garbage can. When he sat down at his desk in English, he hardly heard his teacher's voice as he struggled to keep the anger from his eyes.

"Don't worry none about that," his mother comforted him while they washed dishes together after dinner. "You just be the best you can be, and in the end it will all work out."

"I'm not ever dating any white girls," Sebi added. "Not after what happened to you."

Ralph nodded, and although he kept friendships with all races, he never asked a white girl on a date after that. As he studied the scriptures, though, the anger drained from him. He knew that Father in Heaven was no respecter of persons and that eventually people would be respected just because they were people.

He continued to attend church with his brother and mom, and his dad appeared to be ever further away from them. One day after church, when Ralph and Sebi were sixteen, his mother told the boys the news that they had been half-expecting for several years. She said that she and their dad were getting a divorce. Ralph and Sebi sat on either side of their mother on the fur blanket, hugging her.

"It's okay, Mom. You know, you've always taught us right," Ralph comforted her. "We're going to live the best lives we can, for you and Dad."

"Don't you worry at all, Mom," Sebi added. "We'll

always be here for you." Sebi held her hand. "We'll make you proud of us, and I want you to know I'm planning to go on to college."

Their mother smiled and squeezed Sebi's hand.

Ralph loved his dad, and he would miss him. Ralph hadn't been able to see him much lately, though he still had hopes that some day his father would join the Church. Inside, he felt a growing happiness and completeness. "There's something I want to tell you, Mom," Ralph added. He hugged her around the shoulder. "I want to go on a mission when I'm out of high school."

She blew her nose into a tissue. "You boys are the best thing that ever happened to me."

"Is there anything we can do to help you?" Ralph asked.

"You just did," she said and smiled.

The brothers often played football on weekends on the stretch of grass outside the alligator farm or behind the high school with twenty other guys, and that's where Ralph and Sebi began their missionary work in their senior year. After a game, tall, skinny James Baisden sauntered over to Ralph and Sebi. "Good game, you two." James was respected as one of the most popular guys at school.

"You ever play basketball?" Ralph asked.

James nodded, flipping back his long blond hair, his trademark, which hung in waves to his shoulders.

"We play church ball," Ralph said.

Sebi added, "You want to join the team?"

After church basketball, Ralph told James, "We're going to the Mormon Church tomorrow morning."

"You want to come with us?" Sebi offered.

Ralph really didn't think James would be interested because he knew this new friend had tampered with alcohol and drugs, but James surprised him. "Yeah, I do. Sounds all right."

At church, Ralph watched James's eyes fill up several times during sacrament meeting and as he listened to a small Primary girl sing. James was ready to be baptized before he received the lessons, but Ralph invited the missionaries to his house, where James took all six discussions in two weeks. Ralph baptized him at the Jacksonville Stake Center, and Sebi bore his testimony.

Ralph had received the director's award in band and been selected as high school band lieutenant. In his senior year, he was chosen as band captain, and it was in band that Ralph continued his missionary efforts.

He first noticed Bill because he sat so quietly in his chair with his trombone in his lap, keeping his pale eyes focused on the music stand. His jeans were frayed on the bottom, and his T-shirt was faded and stretched thin.

"How you doing?" Ralph asked him before the instructor entered.

Bill looked up, as if surprised to be spoken to, and every day after that, they talked as they waited for class to begin.

One day Bill asked, "Do you go to church?"

Ralph smiled. "Sure, you want to come with me?"

Bill paused for a second, smiled, then nodded.

Ralph proudly picked him up in his and Sebi's newly purchased Toyota Corolla, an older model with a hatchback for chucking basketballs and bookbags into. Bill agreed to listen to the missionaries. When Ralph arrived at one discussion, Bill was floundering, unable to make up his mind about joining the Church. But after Ralph bore his testimony, Bill accepted the challenge, and Ralph baptized him two months later.

Ralph also met Wendy in band, another shy person

who seemed to hide behind her flute. When his band staged the "Rock-a-thon" in February to raise money for equipment, he collected pledges for donations. Then he "rocked" in a rocking chair for eight hours, while he laughed, ate chips with band members, and told Wendy about the Mormon Church. Ralph invited the missionaries to his house for the discussions, and he baptized Wendy one month later.

Together Ralph and Sebi also fellowshipped a thirty-year-old couple investigating the Church. After many discussions, the couple accepted the challenge. Sebi baptized the husband, and Ralph baptized the wife. When ward members slapped Ralph on the back and congratulated him on what a fine missionary he was, he simply smiled and shrugged his shoulders, while inside, he glowed because baptizing his friends had made him terribly happy.

Sebi finished his senior year as company commander in the ROTC, graduated with a 3.3 GPA, and received a scholarship to attend Kemper Military College in Booneville, Missouri. Ralph served as seminary president in his senior year and graduated with honors with a 3.5 average.

Ralph felt complete with the gospel, but one worry kept nagging at him, and he expressed it to his priests quorum advisor one Sunday before he was to leave on his mission. "How am I ever going to meet the kind of woman I want for a wife?" he asked, still remembering the hurt from his attempt to date a white girl. "I want to marry a black girl, but what if I can't ever find one who's a member of the Church and has my standards? I'm afraid there aren't very many around, you know."

His quorum advisor put his arm around Ralph. "You have lived such a good life, and you're such a shining example to everyone. If you remain faithful on your mission, I promise that the Lord will provide you with an eternal mate, and she'll have the same goals as you. You'll go on to live a happy life."

Ralph tucked the advice in a corner of his mind, trusted the Lord, and prepared to leave for the Massachusetts Boston Mission.

When Ralph and his mother said good-bye to Sebi at the airport, before Sebi was to leave for Kemper College, Ralph chuckled, "No one's ever beaten us, you know, not since Robbie."

Sebi smiled. "Yeah, we sure double-teamed him."

"We've always stuck together." Ralph looked at the ground, then into his brother's eyes. "I don't think I could have made it without you and Mom."

"I'm going to miss you, Ralph."

Ralph and his mother hugged Sebi as the flight attendant announced departure of the flight.

Ralph served faithfully in the Massachusetts Boston Mission and was called to be the assistant to the mission president. Three months into his mission, he met Tracey Graham, a black, University of Montana student from Missoula, who was visiting her sister in Boston. Ralph couldn't help but remember his mother's constant adage about reaping and sowing. He and Tracey wrote letters for fifteen months, and upon completion of his mission, they were married in the Atlanta Temple. The promise made before his mission had been fulfilled.

POSTSCRIPT: Ralph attended Brigham Young University with a multicultural scholarship. He also taught at the Missionary Training Center.

After Kemper Military Junior College, Sebi studied at Northeastern University in Boston. He became second lieutenant in the core of engineers in the army reserves. Sebi met and married Erica Lane, a graduate of MIT in engineering. Both received their endowments and planned a temple marriage in Atlanta.

Above: Patty Amos, right, and Jera
Rucker, left, at Halloween party
after Patty had come home following her bone-marrow transplant

Photos of Patty during ninth grade

"I'M READY NOW"

PARENTS
Susan and James Allen

LOCATION OF STORY
Ajo, Arizona

The sore on Patty's foot looked nasty. She wondered if it could be a spider bite? As it reddened and swelled, Patty's mom picked up some antibiotics for her, which helped, but Patty displayed other strange symptoms over the next few weeks. When she grew very tired and it became difficult for her to breathe, her mom took her to the Arizona Community Clinic in Ajo for a blood test.

The doctor there sent her to the Phoenix Children's Hospital for more blood tests and a spinal tap. He indicated that he suspected something worse than a spider bite. The results of the tests confirmed that sixteen-year-old Patty was suffering from an acute form of nonlymphoblastic leukemia, or cancer of the blood. Mutant cancer cells were multiplying rapidly and crowding out the good cells made by her bone marrow.

Patty felt weak and dizzy when she heard the results, but since she didn't know a lot about leukemia, she didn't know what to expect. "Maybe I'll just take some medicine for a while and then get better," she told her mother.

At the Phoenix Children's Clinic, she met several other young people with cancer, and many had almost recovered from the disease. She met Peter Fisher, a nineteen-year-old boy with a brain tumor, who was also a Mormon. He had endured leukemia for at least two years and would receive a bone marrow transplant in Tucson during the summer. His cheerful attitude reassured her. "You can do it too," he said. "We can get well."

While at the hospital, her dad gave her a priesthood blessing. The doctor decided to operate to place a catheter in her chest through which to inject medicine. As nurses wheeled her down the hall on a gurney, she lay on her back and stared at the ceiling, at the bursts of lights passing overhead. It wasn't the first serious problem Patty had encountered, so she could be tough.

She remembered that when she had been in seventh grade, their house had burned down. They had been living on the Navajo reservation in Northeastern Arizona, where her father had been a teacher for the Bureau of Indian Affairs. Wearing a long satin skirt, velvet blouse, and mocassins, Patty had performed native dances at other schools on the reservation with her sister Crystal and their Navajo friends.

In the end, it was the same Navajo skirt that had caught fire. Her little brother Michael had sneaked into the clothes closet to flick a lighter and watch it glow. The bottom of her skirt accidentally caught fire. Within fifteen minutes the whole wooden house was blazing. The volunteer fire department attached the hose to the wrong side of the truck, and by the time they got it attached the right way, they could only save the house next door.

The next day Patty had reassured her little brothers and sisters. "Don't worry," she said as she squeezed Michael. "Just behave yourselves, and don't whine. See all these sacks of clothes our friends have given us. Reach in and grab something to wear to school."

Everything had burned—everything except one old, stubborn pepper tree in the front of their home. Fire had hollowed it out, and they all thought it was dead, but when spring came, they were surprised to see new branches, with new buds and leaves bursting out.

Patty remembered the pepper tree as they wheeled her into surgery. She could send out new branches too. She could beat leukemia.

While Patty recovered from the surgery to put the tube in her chest, her best friend, Jera Rucker, visited her often. On one trip, Jera brought Patty a present.

"This is a 'heimer.'" She handed Patty a set of crocheted strands of yarn bound together at the top.

Patty smiled and looked puzzled. "Thanks, Jera."

"I call this one a 'rainbow curly,'" Jera said, chuckling. "It's neat because it represents the seven colors of the Young Women values."

"Did you make it?"

"Yes—just for you."

Patty looked around her hospital room. "I know, I'll hang it on my I.V. pole, and then whenever anyone asks about it, I can tell them about the Church."

Patty's hair was her most striking feature, hanging to her waist in golden-brown tresses. She braided it, wrapped it in circles of French twists, frizzed it, tied it with a ribbon in a pony tail, or let it fall like a silky cloak over her shoulders and down her back. She had also styled the hair of her older sister, Sherry, before the prom and the hair of her younger sisters, Crystal, Rachel, and Danita, before school and church. When Patty began chemotherapy, however, she lost all her hair and began to wear hats to cover her bald head.

The physicians in Phoenix sent Patty to the University of California at Los Angeles, where a doctor harvested her bone marrow by injecting needles into her hip in many places and pulling out a liter of bone marrow. He would use this bone marrow transplant later to encourage her body to produce its own healthy blood.

Although Patty was too sore from the bone-marrow harvest to hike, she still attended the Church girls' camp at Camp Lomia, located in the mountains near Payson, Arizona, with Jera, who had just had her appendix removed.

When the other girls hiked into the mountains for a two-day solo, the Young Women leaders drove Patty and Jera to the site. As the girls lay in the tent at night, they reminisced and planned for next year's sophomore year at Ajo High School.

"Are you going to play volleyball?" Jera rolled her pillow under her head to prop herself up.

"Yes," Patty said, "and basketball and softball too." She paused, then added, "I still want to march in the band and play clarinet."

"It will be neat. Think of it. You'll be vice president of the school, and I'll be treasurer."

Patty could see millions of stars through the opening in the tent and could smell pine in the air. "Are you going on a mission some day, Jera?"

"I want to."

"Me, too," Patty answered, "and someday I want to marry a really good man in the temple."

"Yes, and I want a family, but I want an education too."

Patty sniffed, then said, "You know, I'll be over this in a little while, Jera. I'm going to get well."

"I know."

Several girls were still by the campfire, singing a Michael McLean song. The wind carried their high, clear voices: "The friend who helps you see where your choices will lead is the kind of friend you never want to lose . . . "[1]

"You know something, Jera?"

"What?"

"Some things you can lose, and it doesn't matter. Like when our house burned down, it was bad, but you can replace those things." She paused, then added, "But I wouldn't ever want to lose a friend . . . like you."

"You never will." Jera squeezed Patty's arm.

At the end of July, Patty flew to the UCLA Hospital for another bone-marrow harvest. She received a letter from Jeanie Dalton, a fourteen-year-old LDS girl in Seattle, Washington, who also had leukemia. They shared their worries and their hopes through the mail.

Patty received bad news from Peter Fisher's family, the boy she had met in the Phoenix Children's Clinic. He had died during his transplant in Tucson. They informed her that Peter had written in his journal before he died that it was time to go and that he was ready. He had written that he was doing fine and that he would be going to the other side to serve his mission.

"I can't believe that Peter felt he was ready," she said to her mother. "I'll miss Peter. It's terrible." She clenched her fists and wiped her eyes. "But I'm going to get well. I won't give in."

Patty received additional chemotherapy to prepare her for the upcoming transplant at UCLA. Her family and friends prayed it would be successful. Her father gave her many blessings, while the whole community of Ajo prayed for her, including both Mormon bishops and Protestant ministers.

The transplant went well, but as Patty started to recover, she developed infection through the catheter that went into her chest, and she was placed in isolation.

After she was allowed out of isolation, she met Adrian Vallejo, a seventeen-year-old boy who had undergone a transplant. They got together in their rooms, told jokes and laughed, put puzzles together, colored, watched videos, and played games.

One doctor asked the receptionist at the desk on Patty's floor, "What's the difference between the patients on the other side of the hall and Patty's side? The other side is depressed and sorrowful," he pointed out, "while they're always laughing in Patty's room."

Patty answered those who asked her, "It's my beliefs that make the difference." She passed out several copies of the Book of Mormon. She shared the gospel with those who would listen: the nurses, doctors, even a man who fixed their car tires.

Patty developed blood clots in her bladder. The pain was like constant knife stabs in her lower abdomen, and it lasted for three months, from August to October. She grew discouraged and cried a lot. "I'm afraid I'm never going to get out of here," she told her mom.

"I think it's probably just a question of time, Patty," her mother replied.

"But when I think of Joseph Smith when he was a boy and had that abscess on his leg, I think it's not so bad. If he could endure pain like that, so can I."

During that time Jera didn't forget Patty. She prayed for her and wrote at least four letters a week. She telephoned her too and flew to California twice to stay with her in the hospital. She cheered her up and made her laugh again.

Finally, after cauterization, the bleeding in her bladder slowed. She was released from UCLA Hospital and flew home to spend a week in the Phoenix Children's Hospital. Since she was still bleeding, she would have to continue to have blood transfusions once a week.

She was released on Halloween night to go home. Her home seemed noisy and busy after three months spent mostly in isolation. Her little brothers Robert and Michael climbed on her bed, rubbed the fuzz on the top of her head, and snuggled next to her. Her baby brother, Jason, just one year old, crawled over the folds in the blanket and flopped onto his side, grabbing his toe to chew. Patty laughed and cried at the same time. "This is the best medicine," she said.

Her leukemia went into remission. When it stopped spreading, her family cheered, laughed, hugged, and cried. During her recovery, Patty continued to complete school assignments, always receiving good grades, and she spent many hours reading novels.

In the late fall Patty received news that Jeanie Dalton, who also had leukemia, had died of pneumonia, following her transplant. Patty shut her moist eyes. She tried hard not to dwell on it, but then Adrian Vallejo died too, near Patty's birthday. She banged her fist on her bed and cried. It was as if someone had plucked off two more branches from her pepper tree.

Jera visited her regularly during November and December, telling Patty jokes and encouraging her. Jera drove Patty to a pizza parlor for her birthday on December 20.

"Do you remember when we met?" Jera asked.

"Yes, the Fourth of July, just before sixth grade."

Jera smiled. "Uh huh. We were at the town parade. I was the only Mormon girl in my grade, and I was really excited because you had moved in."

They drove to the town square where they had met.

The tall pine tree in the middle of the square was decorated with hundreds of blinking Christmas lights. Palm trees swayed at the sides as though doing homage to the holiday tree. There was the P.D. Store, Phelps, the Dodge Store. Nothing had changed. Only Patty felt different.

"I remember you," Jera said. "You had this long, long hair." She motioned down to the floor of the car.

Patty laughed and said, "Not that long, but you were tall and skinny. You were wearing shorts, and your legs were strings."

Jera made a face as she reached in the back seat. "I have a present for you." She handed her a shirt with an upside-down head, which read, "Normal is boring."

Patty roared and slipped it over her head. "I'm going to make it. I'm going to beat this."

"I know," came the soft answer.

On January 2, when Patty went to the Children's Clinic, the doctor discovered she was out of remission. The leukemia had returned.

Patty felt a rush of heat to her head, and her forehead broke out in beads of sweat. She dropped her face in her palms and cried, "I didn't expect this. All those months in isolation, all that pain—and all I got was two months of remission." It was the first time she wondered if she would really get well again.

The doctor placed another Broviac tube in Patty's chest, and she began chemotherapy again. He warned the family that once a person went out of remission, chemotherapy usually wouldn't work so well. It didn't work with Patty.

The doctor told her parents that there was one last thing they could try. They could inject her with a combination of powerful chemicals, but after three injections, he stopped the treatment because Patty developed painful blood clots in her legs as a result.

The blood clots continued to grow worse each week. At first Patty could hobble around at home if someone took her arm. Soon she could not even let her legs dangle off the side of the bed because the rushing blood shot pain down her legs like heated pokers. Her parents began moving her about in a wheelchair with her legs tucked up on the seat.

One day she had a visit from her older sister, Sherry, who was married and had a baby.

Patty looked in the hand mirror and straightened her hat. She was bald again. Even the short brown fuzz had fallen out because of the last chemotherapy. She was down to ninety-five pounds, and her face had developed shadows and hollows in her cheeks, under her eyes, and in her chin. Her shoulders bent over like a tree that had forever been blown and pushed downward by the wind. "I don't look too much like a movie star, do I," she said, smiling.

Smiling too, Sherry sat on the edge of her bed and said, "You know, I've been thinking a lot lately. Do you remember our mobile home in Greenbrier, Arkansas?"

"We had chickens—little, yellow fuzzy things."

"And ducks. Even geese."

Patty added, "Remember Rainbow, the cat? She used to sleep with me."

"And the dogs next door kept trying to get the ducks and geese—"

"So we took them inside." Patty laughed, remembering that life years ago.

Sherry threw back her head and chuckled. "All of us in that little mobile home."

"But it wasn't crowded."

Sherry's smile faded. "No, it wasn't crowded."

Patty called to the kitchen from her bedroom. "Oh, Mom, remember Sassy? Our dog on the reservation when I was just starting school?"

Her mother wiped her hands on a hand towel as she walked into the bedroom. "Of course, I remember Sassy. How could I forget her."

"Remember we lost her and then found out the dog catcher had her. I'll never forget it. I wish we could have bought her back."

"I know, I know." Patty's mother sat down on a wooden chair. "I know it's hard to believe, but your dad had no work for that summer when school was out, and we honestly couldn't afford the thirty-five dollars to buy her back." She rubbed her hand across Patty's forehead. "I'm sorry."

"It's okay. Maybe I'll see Sassy soon."

Sherry looked down and then shut her eyes.

Patty smiled and took her sister's hand. "Don't worry, Sherry. I'm willing to do what God wants now."

Patty's mother contacted the Make-a-Wish Foundation, a nonprofit organization that finances the wishes of children and adolescents who suffer from life-threatening illnesses.

"If I had one wish," Patty mused, "it would be to go back to the Sacred Grove, to Carthage Jail, and see the Church history sites." However, Patty was in too much pain and too weak to handle that. So she thought some more and then decided. "I want to go to Salt Lake City and meet a General Authority and do baptisms for the dead."

The administrator of the Make-a-Wish Foundation told Patty's mother that he found it hard to believe that she had not asked to meet a movie star or to go to Disney

World. "Why would she want to meet some old man?" he asked.

That's exactly what Patty wanted, and the Foundation fulfilled that wish. On April 10, Patty, her whole family (except Sherry, who was unable to go), and Jera flew to Salt Lake City. She met President Thomas S. Monson, Second Counselor in the First Presidency; Elder L. Tom Perry, of the Council of the Twelve; and Virginia H. Pearce, First Counselor in the Young Women's general presidency. Patty visited Temple Square and enjoyed a carriage ride around the city. She spoke at the Orchard Sixth Ward in Bountiful and told everyone to take care of their bodies, and she met with a twelve-year-old boy with both leukemia and spina bifida. She told him, "Have courage. You can still accomplish a lot."

Jera and Patty's sister Crystal decided to do baptisms for the dead with Patty. Being baptized was a bigger problem for Patty because she couldn't stand without searing pain in her legs, but she wanted to try. Her father carried her delicate body into the water and gently placed her down. Patty stood there. Color flushed her cheeks. To the surprise of everyone, she felt no pain. Instead, her body felt soaked in peace. It nestled around her, lifted her up. She was dipped under the water, strong arms supporting her thin shoulders, then back up. The water slipped from her face like silk. She stood there and completed ten baptisms for the dead, and she felt no pain in her legs at all.

"There are many sisters waiting for you now, Patty," her dad confided. "Your ten, and Jera's and Crystal's ten. I feel inspired that you will be their teacher."

Back home in Ajo, Patty watched Crystal getting ready to go to the band concert. She wore Patty's black-and-white jumpsuit. Patty styled her sister's hair so soft curls feathered around her cheeks, then she pulled the hat down further over her own bald head. She felt the hollows in her cheeks sinking deeper, her whole body sucking in like quicksand.

She watched four-year-old Robert and baby Jason roll on the floor together. Robert clung to Jason's chubby leg as he tried to crawl away.

Suddenly Patty blurted out, "But I want to see them grow. I just want to be here to see them do things for the first time." She dropped her head into her folded arms and cried. "That's the part I'll miss."

Her mother hugged her tightly. "I know."

"But I'm ready, I think. I remember when Peter died, he said he knew it was time to go. I never understood how he could say that. Now I understand, but I don't know how I could do this if I didn't know where I was going."

They clung together and cried.

"It won't be long now," Patty whispered.

"Your grandpa will be there to greet you."

"And Sassy will be jumping on me, and my friends—Jeanie, Peter, and Adrian—will be there." Patty smiled through tears. "We'll probably have a big party."

"And you'll teach those sisters you did baptisms for."

"Yes, people will be waiting." Patty took a long look at the ceiling. "I feel I've learned so much this past year, about faith and patience, about prayer. I wouldn't trade everything I've gone through this year. I wouldn't trade it for anything. I feel ready to go now, but I'll be back, Mom. I'll be back in the Millennium."

Less than two months later, in July, Patty Amos passed away quietly in her home, surrounded by family.

---

1. "Be That Friend" (Shining Star Music, ASCAP, 1986).

INDEX

ABOUT THE AUTHOR

Barbara Lewis is the author of the best-selling book *The Kid's Guide to Social Action,* as well as *Kids with Courage.* She teaches fourth through sixth grades at Jackson Elementary School in Salt Lake City, Utah. She has won over a dozen major awards for her writing and teaching, such as *Parenting*'s Reading Magic Award, ALA Book List for Reluctant Readers, and Distinguished Alumnus Award from the University of Utah.

Some of the true stories in Barbara's books have come from her experiences with her students. Her books and her students' projects have been featured on CBS and CNN news and in over seventy magazines and newspapers, including *The Wall Street Journal, Newsweek,* and *Family Circle.*

A member of The Church of Jesus Christ of Latter-day Saints, Barbara has served in her ward as a teacher, a president in the Young Women's organization, and in the Relief Society presidency. Barbara and her husband, Lawrence, have four children, Mike, Andrea, Christian, and Samuel.